CODING, ANIMATION AND GAMES WITH SCRATCH

Sumita Mukherjee
www.wizkidsclub.com

More books from WIZKIDS CLUB:

Stem/Steam Activity Books: 6-10 Year Kids

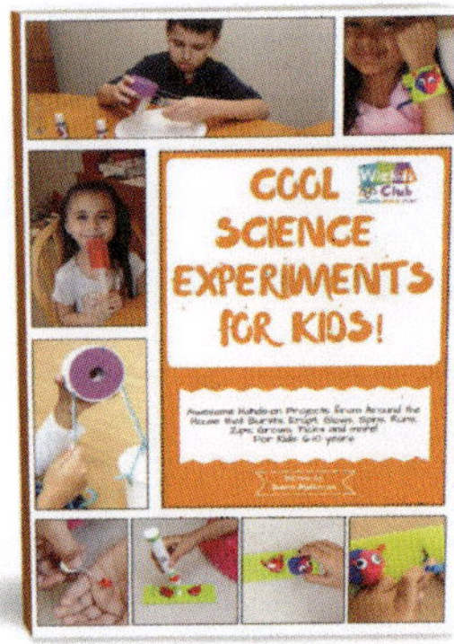

COOL SCIENCE EXPERIMENTS FOR KIDS

Grades: 1-5
Skill level: Beginner
Time: 19 projects; 30-40 minutes each

COOL SCIENCE EXPERIMENTS FOR KIDS is an amazing book full of hands-on activities. With awesome Science, Technology, Engineering, Art and Math project ideas, it is an easy way to entertain any bored kid! A great way to acquire 21st century skills and STEM learning.

Inside this book you will find projects on Simple Machines, Merry-go Round, Spinning Doll, Exploding Bottle, Safe Slime, Architecture, Crafts, Games and more!

Loads of fun with projects that burst, glow, erupt, spin, run, tick and grow!

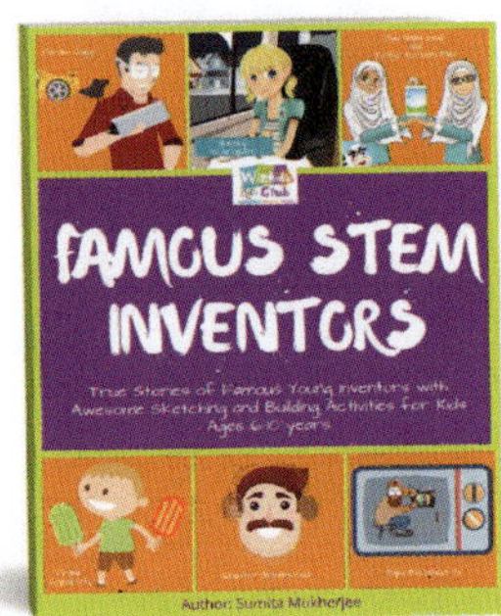

FAMOUS STEM INVENTORS

Grades: 1-5
Skill level: Beginner
Time: Reading time: 15-20 mins and activities of 20-30 minutes each.

FAMOUS STEM INVENTORS introduces kids to the world's most famous young inventors in the field of S.T.E.M. (Science, Technology, Engineering and Math). All things that we enjoy are a product of brilliant minds, scientists and engineers. This book imparts information that is interesting and engaging to young boys and girls between 6-10 years of age.

STORY OF INVENTORS: Kids will be transported to the fascinating world of famous creators and learn about their first inventions: Glowing paper, Popsicle, Windsurf board, Television, Earmuffs and more. The book arouses their natural curiosity to be inspired from their role models.

DESIGN PROCESS: It showcases the Engineering Design Process behind every invention. Highlights what they invented and how they invented, thereby, revealing the steps to all new discoveries.

SKETCHING AND DESIGNING ACTIVITY: It encourages kids to sketch and design their own ideas through the design activity. This book prompts kids to think creatively and it arouses their natural curiosity to build, make and tinker.

STEAM AHEAD! DIY FOR KIDS

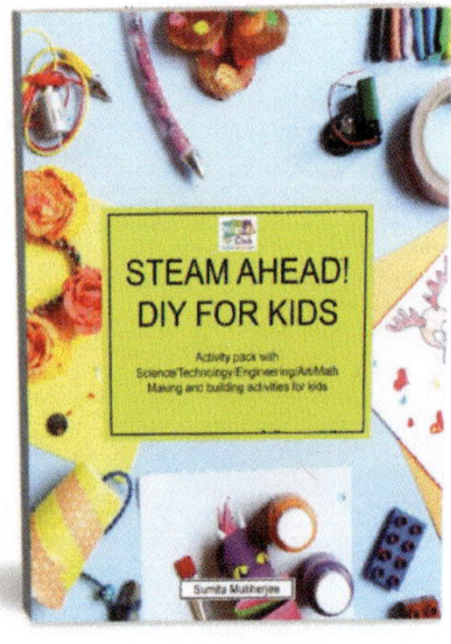

Grades: 1-5
Skill level: Beginner
Time: 21 projects; 30-40 minutes each

STEAM AHEAD! DIY FOR KIDS is an amazing book full of hands-on activities. With awesome Science, Technology, Engineering, Art and Math project ideas, it is an easy way to entertain any bored kid! A great way to acquire 21st century skills and STEM learning.

Inside this book you will find projects on LED cards, dance pads, handmade soaps, bubble blowers, Play-Doh circuits, cloud lanterns, scribbling bots and more!

Awarded 5 stars by READERS' FAVORITE site, Parents, Educators, Bloggers and Homeschoolers.

IMAGINE. BUILD. PLAY.

www.wizkidsclub.com

Publisher: Sumita Mukherjee

Table of Contents

Introduction

What is Scratch?

In movies, whenever the scene involves a programmer, he/she is typing lots of stuff at such a high speed that their fingers are practically a blur. And the character does this for hours!! It is easy to look at such scenes and wonder, “Do I really think that I can reach that level?”

Well, in comes Scratch! Scratch is a unique programming language that is based on blocks – actual blocks. So no need to worry about creating pages of hand-typed code – all you will need to do is drag and drop. Cool, huh?

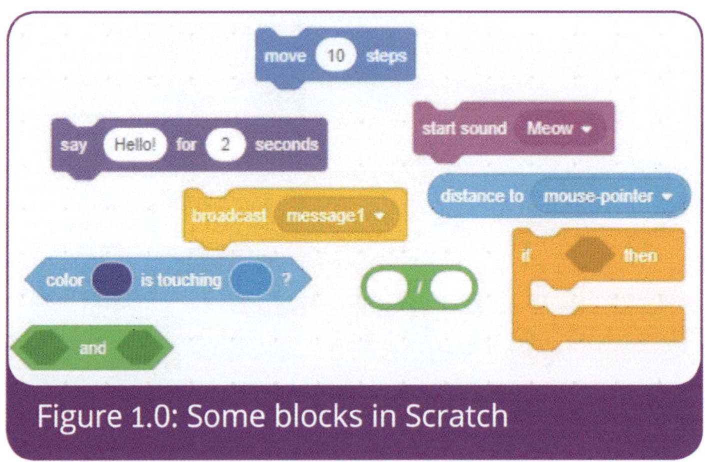

Figure 1.0: Some blocks in Scratch

Why use Scratch?

This is a wonderful place to start for anyone interested in programming or computer science. Like, anyone. Age isn’t a problem and it is available in more than 70 languages.

What can be done with Scratch?

- Games
- Stories
- Animations and more!

License

Once you have created a project and tested it, you can upload it directly to the Scratch website. Members will be able to download, study and even make changes to your project's code.

As a member of the community, of course you can do the same. Feel free to comment on, tag, favourite and love others' projects. Also, if you have any ideas, you can share them!

Now that we are done with all the serious stuff, let us move on!

Opening an Account

Official Scratch Website

Now that you know that Scratch is perfect for you, let's get it onto your computer! In order to do so, we'll do so in this order:

1. Create an account with Scratch.
2. Gain access to the online and offline Scratch editors.

So, anyway, the official Scratch website is:
https://scratch.mit.edu/

Go on! Take a look! You know you want to! The home page should look like this:

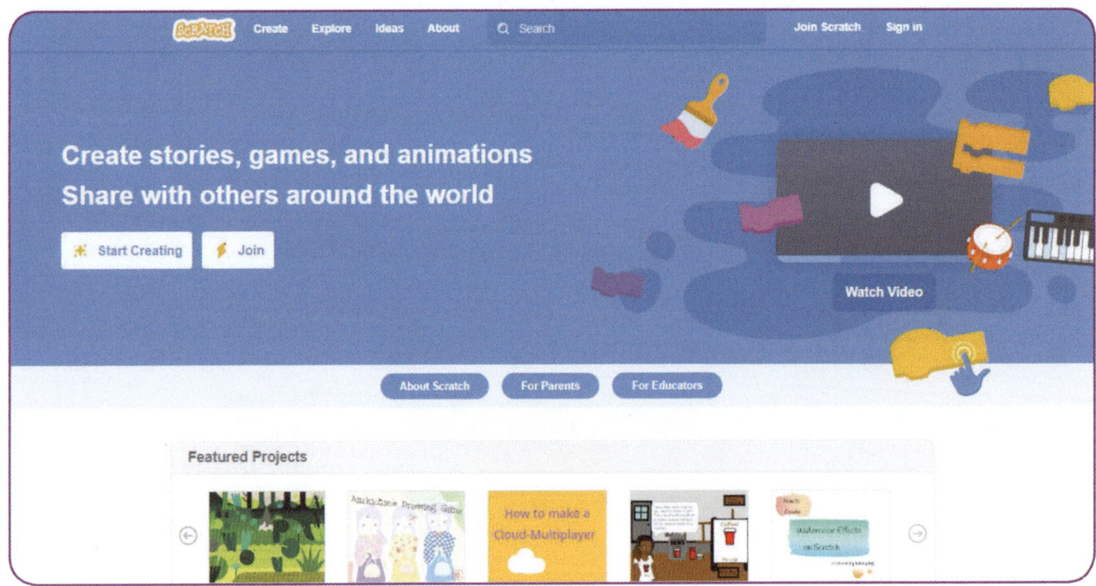

At the top of the homepage is a menu with the options: Create, Explore, Ideas and About.

'Create' shows you how to... create! It has tutorials, so in case you would like video tutorials, you can check this out.

Click 'Explore' if you want to see what other users have created! Seriously, you will be impressed by how cool peoples' creations are!

'Ideas' is where you should go if your creative juices are...frozen. Get them flowing at this point.

For more info about Scratch as a programming language, go to 'About'.

Satisfied? Then let us...

Create an Account with Scratch

First of all, go to the Scratch website. Here's the link again if you are too lazy to scroll up and click it (Yes, I am awesome that way):

https://scratch.mit.edu/

Now click the 'Join us' button. A little form should appear so that the page will look like this:

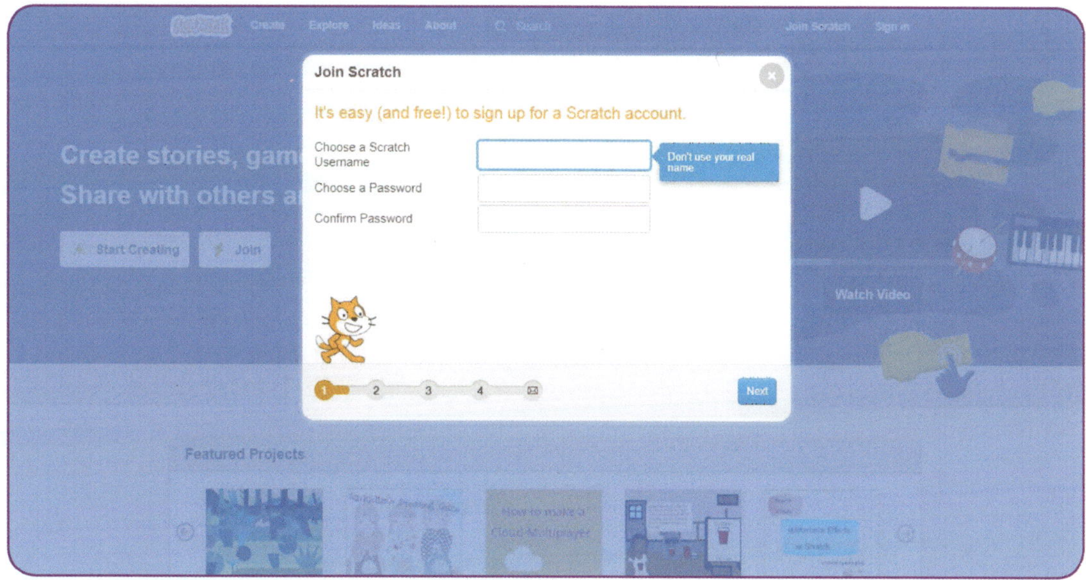

To create an account, you will need:

- A username – something unique and totally you.
- A password – please NOT your birthday or crush or pet.
- The month and year you were born
- Your gender
- Your country
- Your e-mail address (this is important, because scratch will send an e-mail to you to confirm your account. So, yeah, it has got to be legit.)

NOTE: If you ever forget your password or your username, you can go to this link to reset it. **https://scratch.mit.edu/projects/editor/?tutorial=getStarted**

Otherwise, once you have followed the above instructions, congrats!! You now have a Scratch account! So, what next?

The Online Scratch Editor

To get to the online Scratch editor, click this link. The page displayed should look something like this.

One of the pros of using the online editor is you can access your work on any computer. Meaning, if you have a sibling who you believe will one day make the mistake of thinking your computer is thirsty and will give it a drink; your work would still be safe. So, keep that in mind when making the decision.

The Offline Editor

To download this, click this link.

https://scratch.mit.edu/download/scratch2

Go to downloads and click the downloaded file. It will run an installer program. Don't worry about it. All you will have to do is follow the instructions. Once installed, when you open the program, it should look like:

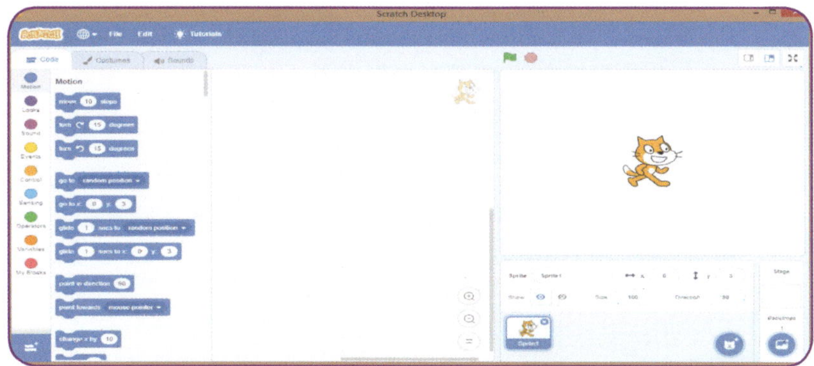

One of the main advantages of using the offline editor is that you won't have to worry much about problems with your internet connection.

Now notice there isn't much of a difference between the online and offline editors. So don't worry much about the choice you make - either way works just as well.

There's a problem though: even though we have successfully opened the editor, you might be wondering what all the buttons are for. Let us get to that.

Getting Started (The Scratch Layout)

At the top of the program are the buttons that appear in every basic program. If you don't know how to use those, ignore them for now. You will see how to use them as we go.

Now the rest of the Scratch layout can be divided into 3 basic parts:

1. The Stage
2. The Sprite List
3. The Blocks Menu

Ever been to a show? It is made up of actors and actresses, a script and the stage. Think of this as a production.

Let us see what each of those is for.

The Stage

Basically, the stage is where you can see the output or results of your code. Check out the part where the cat is in the program. Take a look below to see what I mean.

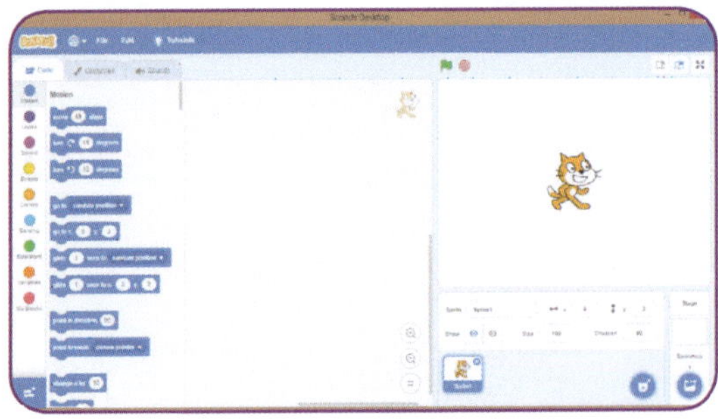

At the top of the page, you will notice a green flag and a red button (makes you think of stop and go, doesn't it!). The flag is what you click to start running the code properly. The red button makes it stop running.

The Sprites list

Cookie batter is awesome - yummy, in fact. But at times, a girl wants a good old chocolate cake. That's when the baking tin is important. By the time we are mixing ingredients, we have already decided if we would like cupcakes, layered cakes or even cookies.

It is the same with sprites, by the time we have started creating code we already know what sprite we would like the code to work on.

Here are some of the sprites that Scratch provides in its program:

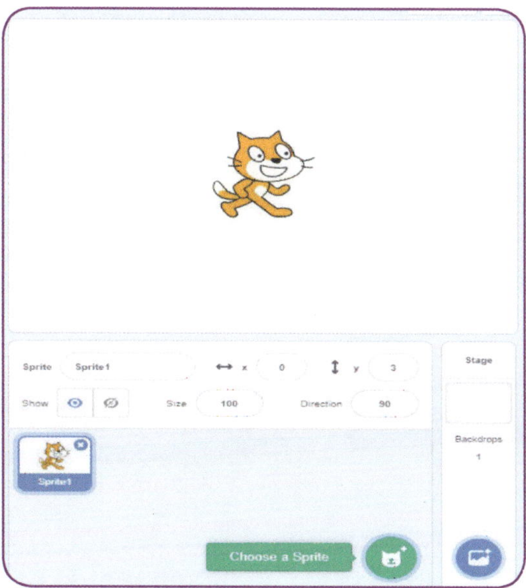

Note: The cat is actually the default sprite.

The Blocks Menu

So, this is the script for the show. As the image below shows, the blocks menu has 3 tabs:

i. **Code** – these are commands that are mostly related to the sprite selected.
ii. **Costumes** – Also related to the sprite. But this time, it has to do with appearance. For example, the cat sprite has one costume walking and the next jumping. This might sound boring, but there's quite a lot we can do with just 2 costumes.
iii. **Sounds** – The sounds associated with the selected sprite. As in, the cat sprite will meow...

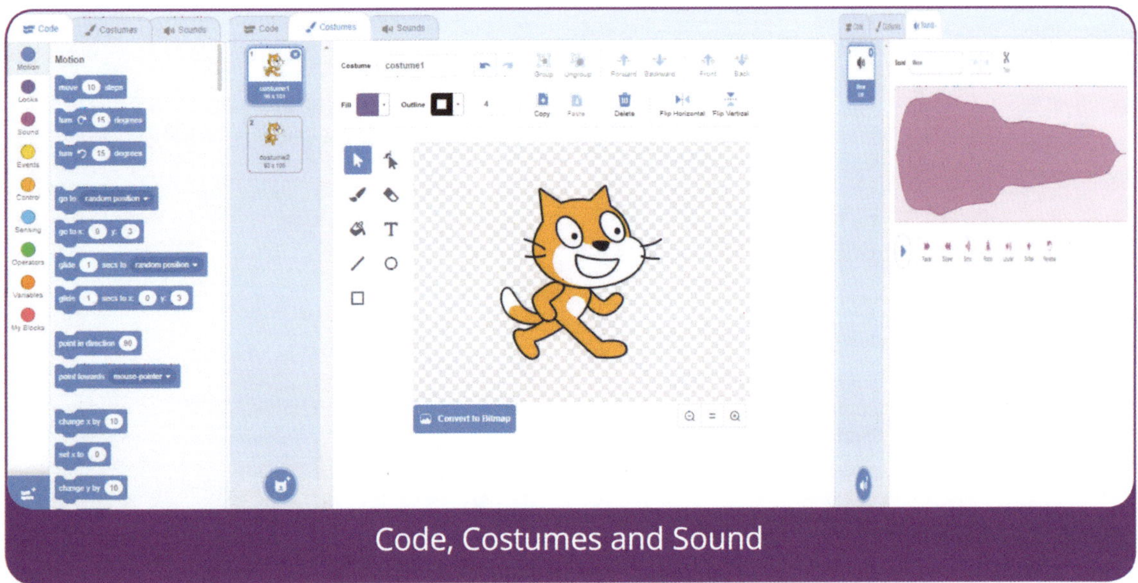

Code, Costumes and Sound

And that's it! Have you understood it all? If not, don't give up. Going through the examples in the coming chapters is likely to help you get it.

TIP: saving and loading programs/games.

Click the 'File' button at the top of the program. Something like this should appear:

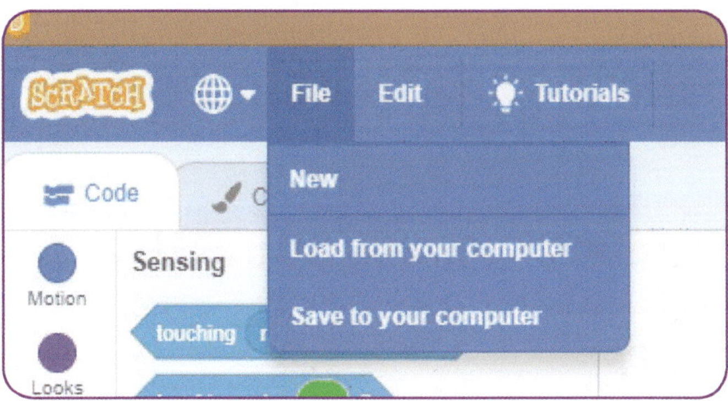

1. New: Click this button to create a new file.
2. Load from your computer: Click this button to load a Scratch program that you had saved earlier.
3. Save to your computer: This is what you click to save a program. It is wise for you to save all your files in a place you can remember and give them names that you can remember. As someone who has made this mistake before, I don't want this to happen to you! Imagine opening and closing more than 10 files just to find the right one. Sounds like fun, huh?

Basics

Statements

Think of Scratch as a programming language that uses puzzle pieces. So each puzzle piece, or block (as the creators call it) is what programmers call a statement. Basically that means that **each puzzle piece or block gives the computer an instruction**.

Even cooler: these puzzle pieces/blocks are organised by shape and colour! This is important because you will know what kind of instruction it is.

Some blocks are like containers; you can put one or more blocks in them. When we do that, we call it a **nested statement**. Like eggs in a basket, get it? Others require user input to make sense. Check out the images below to see what we mean.

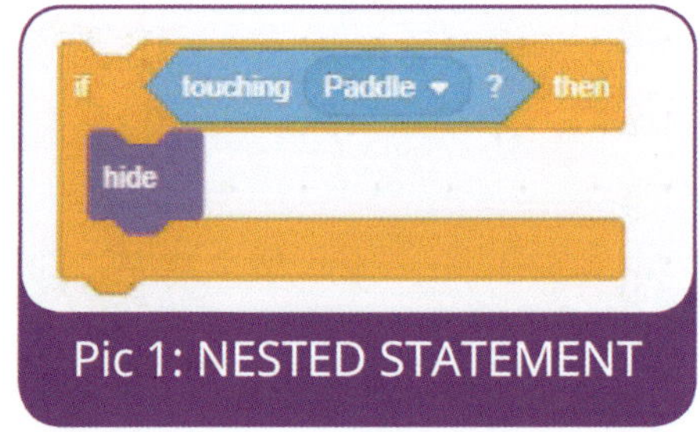

Pic 1: NESTED STATEMENT

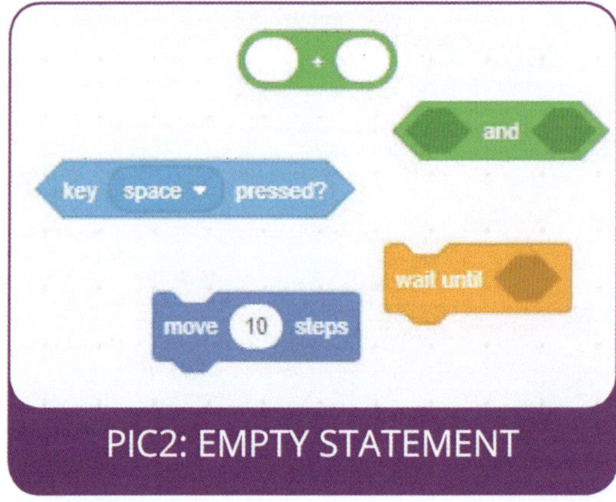

PIC2: EMPTY STATEMENT

Now let us get started on the different types of blocks. To help you find them better in the Scratch program, the colours of the titles in this book will match the colours of the titles in the program. I really hope I am not colour blind because then we will be in big trouble.

The three kinds of blocks below directly affect the sprite chosen.

Motion

Blocks of this kind have to do with the motion or movement of the sprite. Getting a sprite to move up, down, left, right, rotate forwards and backwards can be done here.

When the sprite is loaded to the stage (check the previous chapter if you don't know what those terms mean), its position is x=0 and y=0. It is at the centre of the stage – literally. You know how when plotting a graph, you start counting the point of origin at (0, 0)? Yeah, it is basically like that.

As for what each motion block does, it is basically self explanatory. Some of the blocks have slots to put in data of your choice. If for example, your input to 'change x by __' is 10, undoing the move could be as simple as making the new input -10.

Now let's test it out! We are gonna make an animation!

Animation: Dancing Cat

Become accustomed to the motion blocks that come with Scratch. Learn how to move a sprite to different places on the screen, turn it left or right...

1. Once you open Scratch, 'Cat' is already the default sprite. We'll use it for this animation.

CHOOSE A NEW BACKDROP:

2. Click the 'Choose A Backdrop' Button and select The Backdrop 'Theater 2'.

3. Better now, right? Now click and drag the cat to the spot you want him to be on.

MAKE THE CAT DANCE!

4. In the Events code, look for the block, "when [flag] clicked". It is going to be the first block.

5. In the Control code, get the forever block. It will literally keep the cat dancing forever.

6. In the Motions code, look for the block to the right of this text. Duplicate this block

7. Drag and drop the turn 15 degrees to the right.

8. Out the second glide block here. Then the block that turns to the left.

9. Now all you have to do to run it is click the green flag!

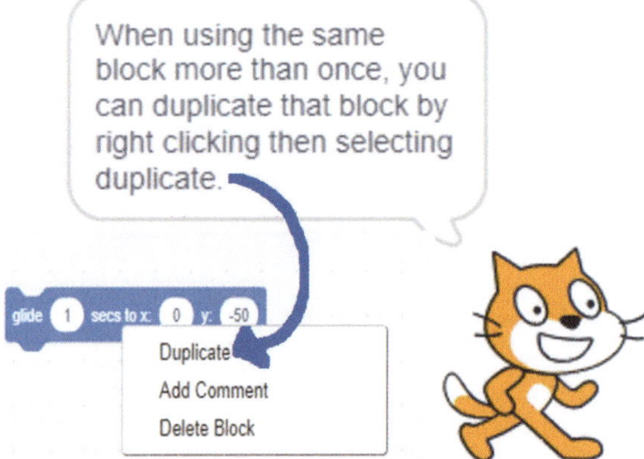

When using the same block more than once, you can duplicate that block by right clicking then selecting duplicate.
glide 1 secs to x: 0 y: -50
Duplicate
Add Comment
Delete Block

This is how the final block of code should look!

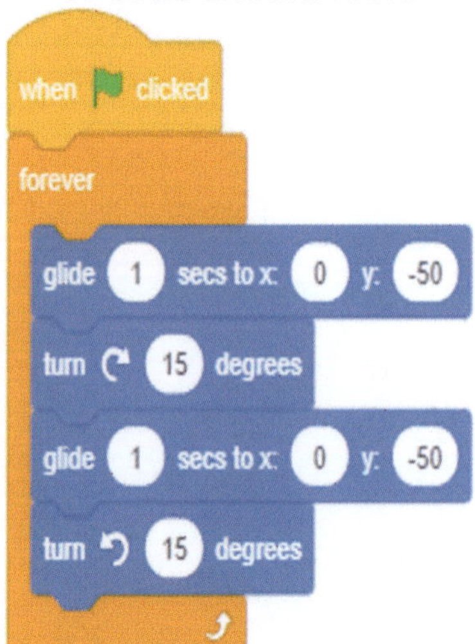

Looks

These blocks have to do with the 'look' of the sprite. Is it talking? What costume is it wearing? What is it saying and for how long? You can take a look at some of the looks blocks.

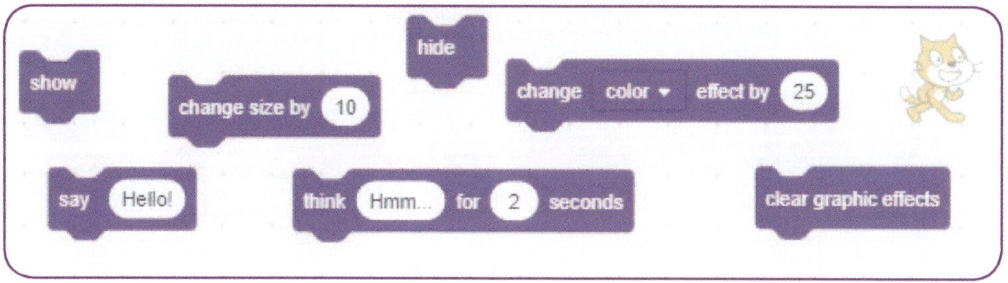

Now, for an activity to show you how some of the looks codes can be done.

ACTIVITY: We are going to make a number of dancing sprites! And this time the dancing will be more sophisticated!

Animation: Sprite Dance-Off

The Cat's dance in the previous chapter was just sad. Here we will take advantage of Costumes and the blocks in looks to make the dance more... sophisticated.

LET'S GET STARTED!

1. Load the previous game "Dancing Sprite".

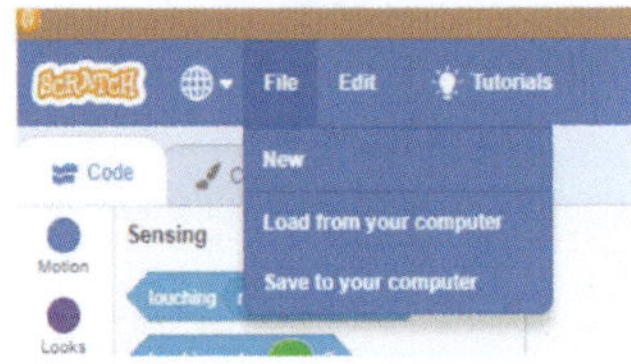

2. Change the backdrop to 'Spotlight'.

3. Add the sprites "Anina Dance' and 'Ballerina'. Drag and drop them on the stage as in the pic below. Make sure the cat is in the middle of the stage. We won't add any code to it, though.

ANINA DANCE:

4. Anina is huuuge! Click (don't drag!) this block. Make sure the number in it is 50%.

SHAKE IT!

5. Get the 'when flag clicked' block from Events.

6. Go to Looks and get the next costume block. Duplicate it so that there are 5 blocks of it.

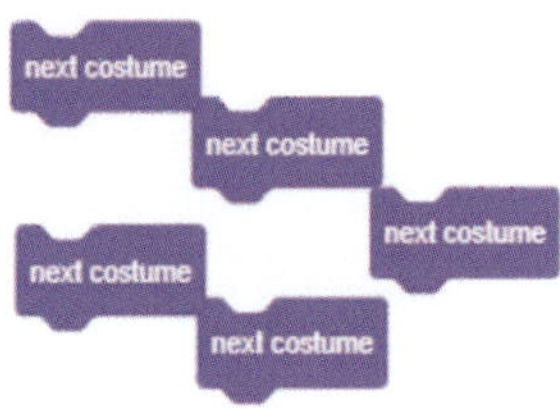

7. The 'wait 1 second' is the last block you will need. 4 such blocks will do. Without this the dancer will move faster that we can see!

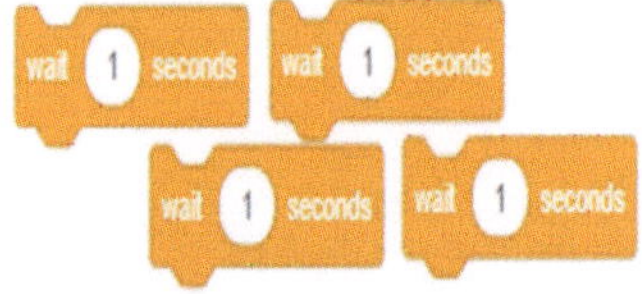

8. Arrange them so that the blocks appear like the blocks just above.

Deleting Backdrop:
Click any of the backdrops in the bottom right corner. In the top left corner, you will see a tab 'Backdrops'. Click it and click the backdrop you want to delete. There will be an 'x' you can click to do so.

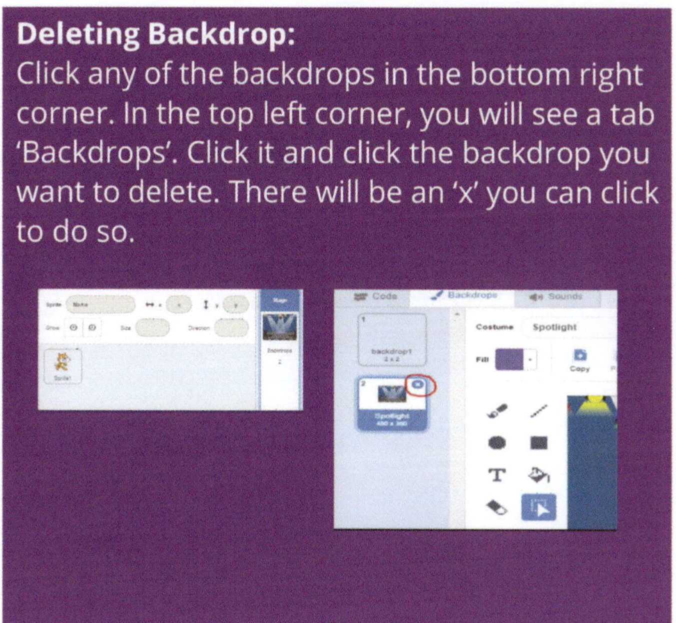

THE BALLERINA:

9. Again, we use the 'when flag clicked' block start.

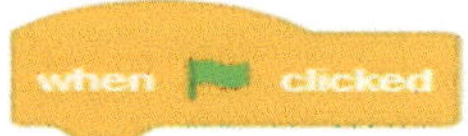

10. Get the 'think Hmm for 2 seconds' block from the Looks blocks.

11. Then get the 'switch costume to' _ dropdown list. We need 4 of these blocks. Each block should have a different costume.

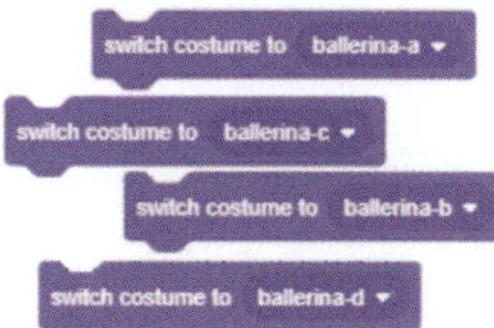

11. Also, we will use the 'wait 1 seconds' block again. 3 of them, that is.

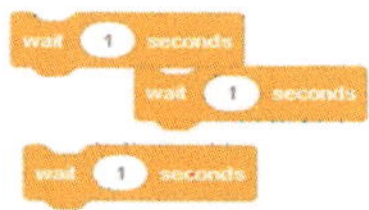

12. Check out the top right pile of blocks to see how they should be compiled.

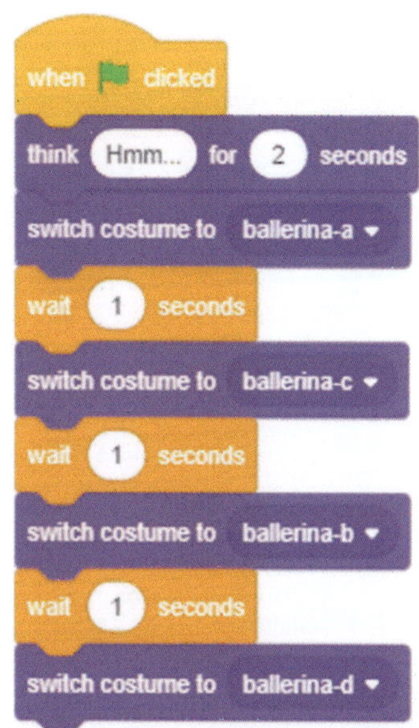

COSTUMES?

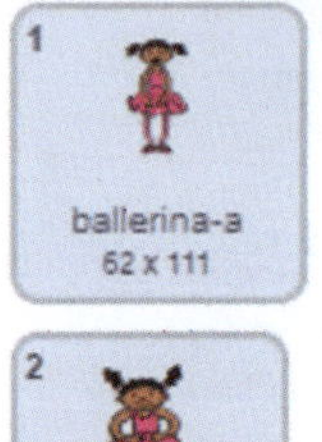

So costumes are basically self explanatory. These are basically the different looks a sprite can change into. The 'blocks next costume' and 'switch costume to' _ can be used to change costumes.

Check out the costumes tab to see the ones specific to the sprite.

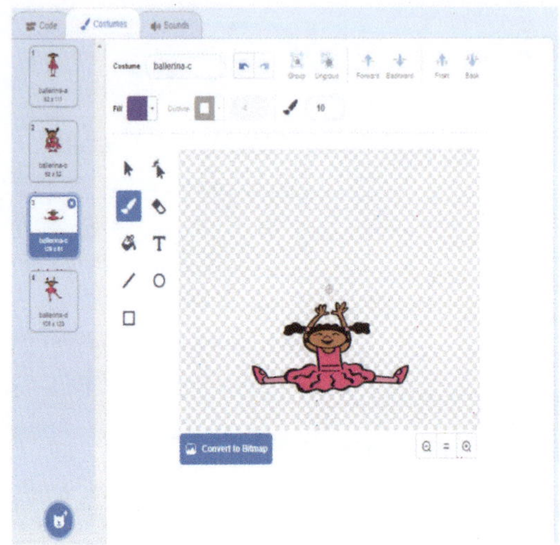

ADDING/DELETING A SPRITE

The bottom right corner of the screen is where to go to add or delete sprites.

Click the button that looks like a cat's head to add a sprite.

To delete one, click the icon for the sprite, then click the close button on the top right corner of the sprite's icon.

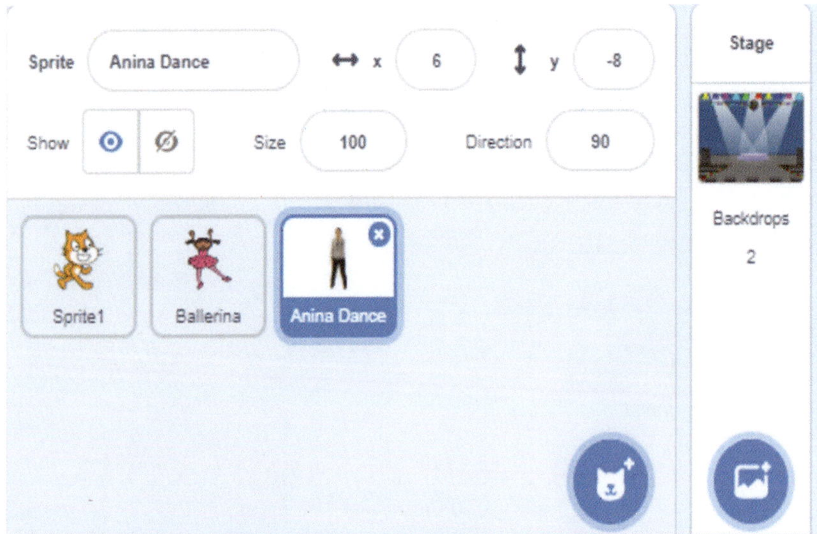

Sounds

Want to associate a sound with a sprite of your choice? This is where you learn how! There 'are a number' of blocks in this section. Take a look at some of them:

Animation: Story-Telling

Combine looks with sounds and motion to tell a story.

1. For starters, let us get the right backdrop: 'Woods'

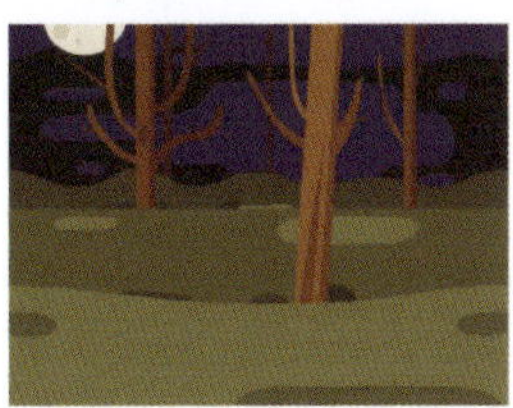

2. The sprites we will use are the Dragon, Princess and the Dove. Delete the cat and add those three to the stage. Set them up like so:

Dragon:

3. We will start with this sprite because dragons are cool. As usual, we start with this block.

4. Next is the show block. This is useful because at times we make the sprites disappear aka 'hide'.

5. Then the wait block.

6. Create 2 'switch costume to' ... blocks.

7. In between them, put the 'play sound' _ until done.
... more on the dragon will come later...

play sound Grunt until done

Princess:

8. Again, the usual start...

9. We add a 'switch costume to' _.

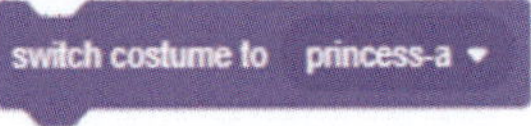

10. Then we give the 'princess a' time-out and give her the 'hide' command.

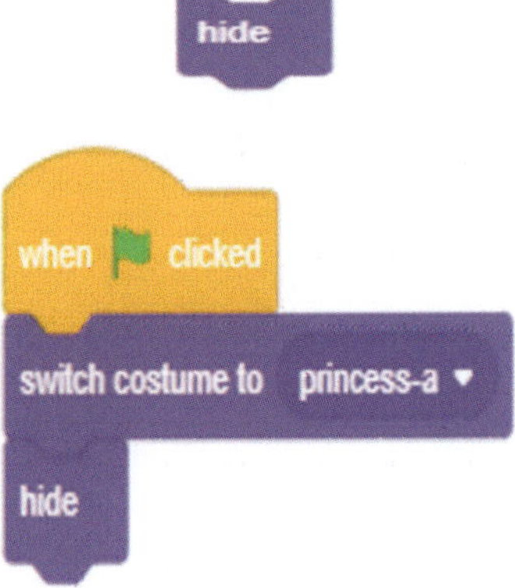

Dove:

12. First, we will start with the usual block. We'll be making two chunks of code so you can duplicate it. Pick one and start filling in the pieces.

13. Get the forever block and drop it under. Remember this makes the block we'll put inside it keep running.

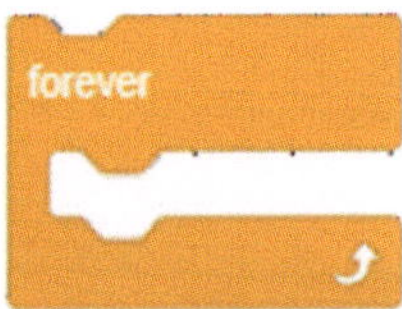

14. Put the 'next costume' block from Looks inside. The Dove has 2 costumes: wings up and wings down.

15. When we add the 'wait 0.5' seconds block to the forever block, the dove will flap it's wings up and down forever. It is flying!

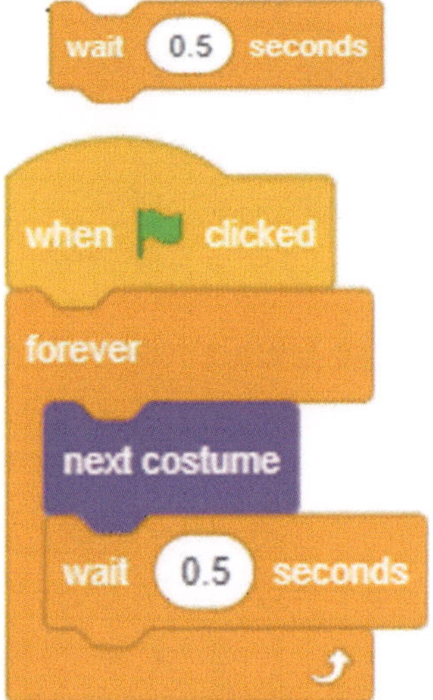

For the second part...

16. Add a show block to the second 'when flag clicked' block.

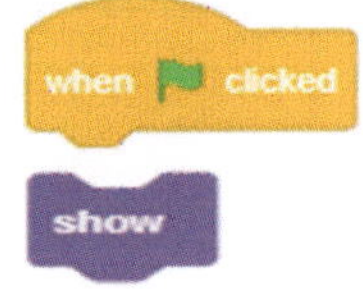

17. This is one talkative dove, so we need to duplicate the 'say' _ for _ seconds block from the Looks block We'll need 6 of them altogether.

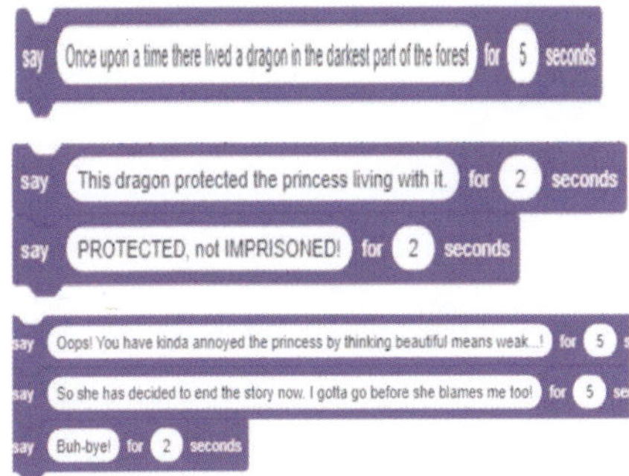

18. You'll need two broadcast [message] blocks from Events.

This is how it should look!

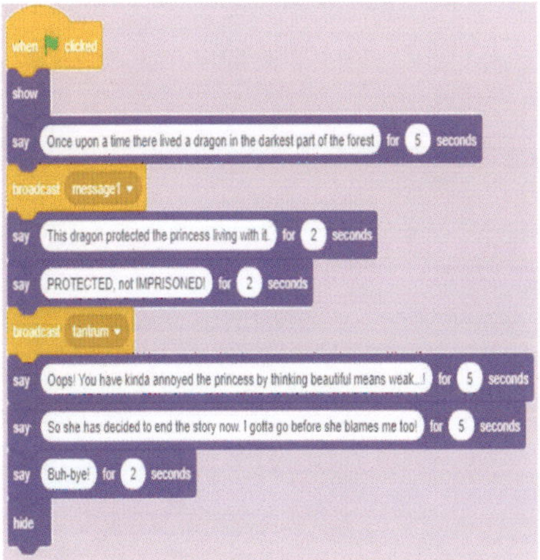

THE BROADCAST BLOCK:
Sometimes we want a chunk of code to run only when something specific has happened. That's when you can use this block to create a broadcast.

- **a)** Click the drop down on the block. Select 'New message'.
- **b)** In the pop-up window, type the name of the event you would like to broadcast.
- **c)** Over the chunk of code you want to run, place a "when I receive [broadcast name]". Use the dropdown list to pick the right option.

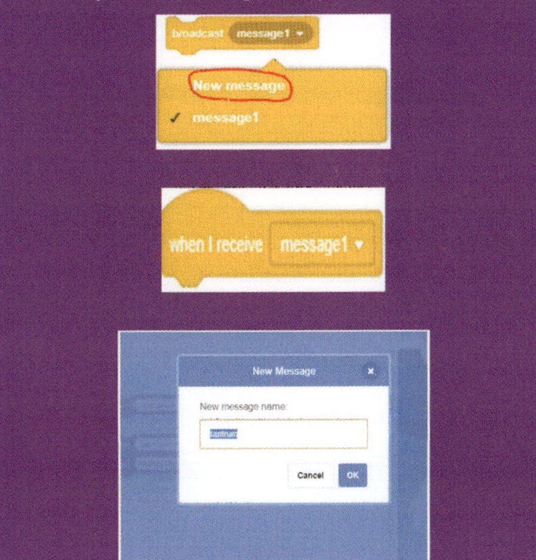

Now that we know about the broadcast blocks, let us add some more to the Princess and the Dragon.

Dragon:

19. Start this chunk with the 'When I receive tantrum'. Remember that the block broadcasting this should exist within the Dove code.

20. We want the dragon to hide at this point.

21. And the oops sound should play until done. Adds pomp to the moment.

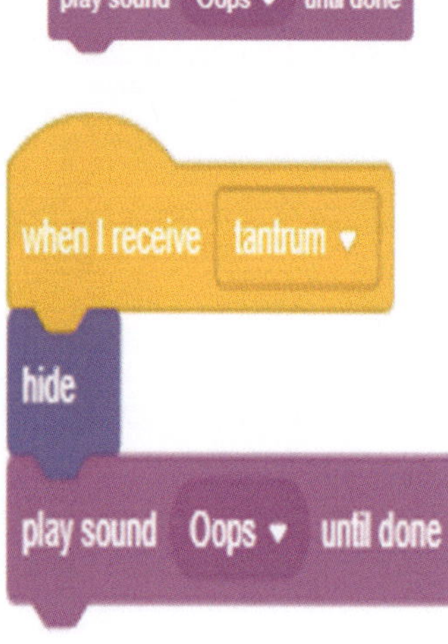

Princess:

22. The second bit of code for princess listens for a 'message1' alert.

23. The princess suddenly appears on the stage thanks to the show block.

24. A graceful pose for our royal highness by switching costumes.

25. And she belts out a few notes for us, because she is musical that way. Use the play sound block.

play sound Singer1 until done

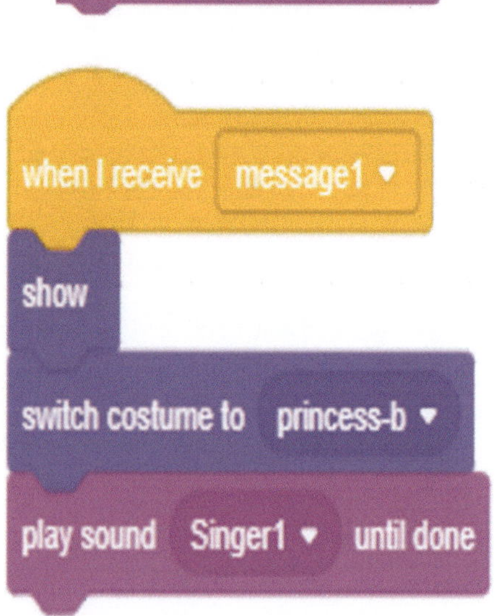

26. At one point in the story, the message 'tantrum' is broadcast.

27. When the princess receives this, she should switch costumes to 'd' (PS. she's the one throwing the tantrum).

28. A 2 second wait...

29. And she switches to another look with the switch costume block.

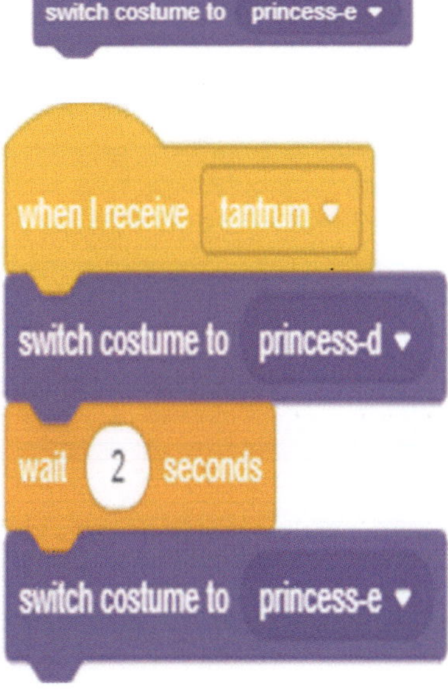

ADDING SOUNDS:

Just as you had to with costumes, check the top left corner for the 'Sounds' tab. In there you can take a look at the sounds that the sprite has. Plus, you can add sounds to the sprite. Here's how:

1. Select the sound button at the bottom left corner in the sounds tab.
2. This should open up a window that shows you all the available sounds. Select one of your choice and you're good to go!

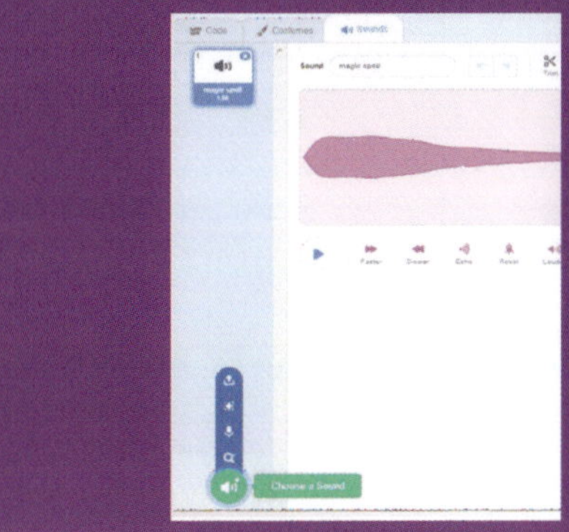

Operators

Operators

1 + 1 = 2

Some of the operators blocks and blocks that they can be used in:

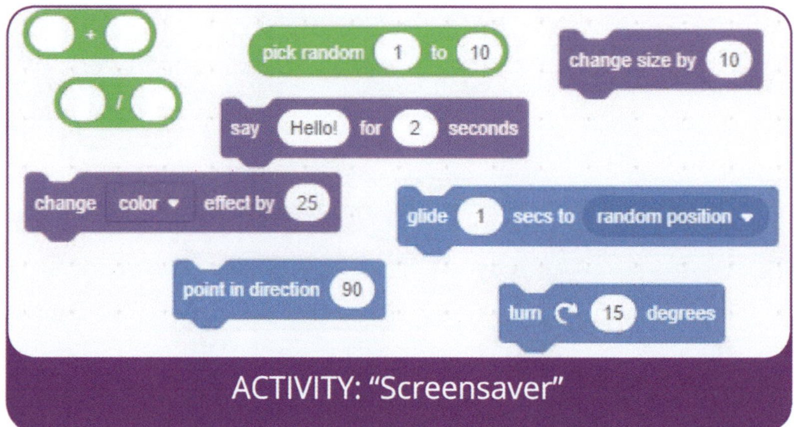

ACTIVITY: “Screensaver”

Screensaver

BECOME FAMILIAR WITH OPERATORS BY CREATING A SCREENSAVER

We will make this animation with minimum effort. How? Load the previous game - The Paddle Game. Then delete the sprite Paddle. Also, change the backdrop to Beach Malibu. Now let us get started:

1. We are going to edit the existing code. Take a look at these 2 images above to see the original code after loading and the final outcome.

2. To remove the if '<touching paddle?>' and all in it, click the if block and drag and drop onto the panel that has the Scratch blocks. Also, remove the first 2 blocks off the pile. That should leave the forever code and its content.

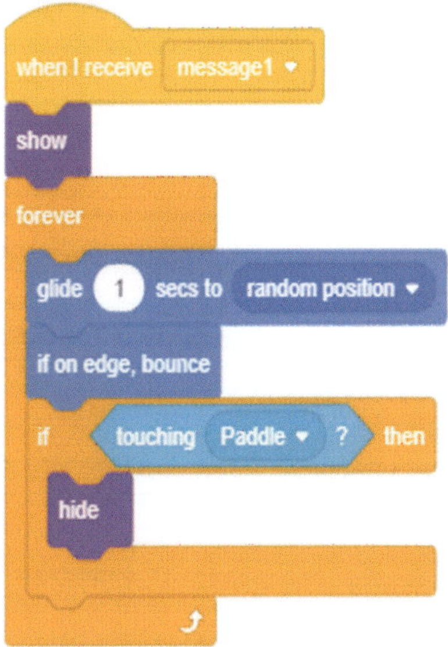

3. Set a 'when flag clicked' block at the top of the forever loop. You can now duplicate this code across all the sprites after deleting the code it previously had.

4. What you have left is the basic code that we will adjust to suit each sprite.

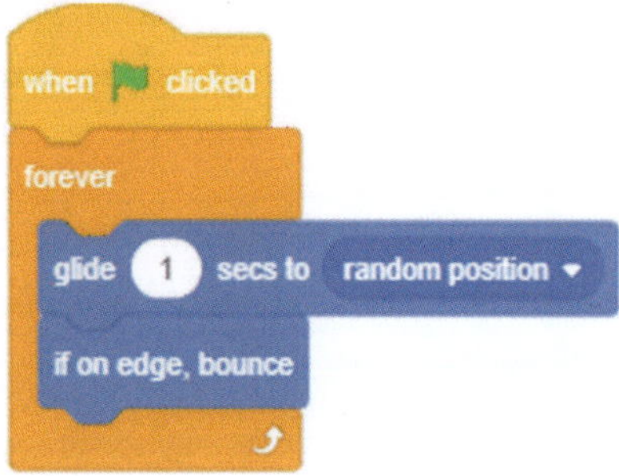

Ball:

1. Go to Operators and get the 'pick random'.
   That will be the input for the 'glide _ seconds to' <'random position'>.

2. Make the next costume from Looks the last block in the forever block.

Basketball:

3. Again we use the pick random block. To spice things up a bit, just make the values different for each sprite.

Beachball:

4. Get the 'change size by' _ block from Looks. In it, we will put another pick random 1 to 10.

5. For the 'glide _ seconds to' <'random position'> we will use 2 operator blocks. In the 'pick random _ to' _, put the addition operator in with values of your choice.

Baseball:

6. From operators we will get 3 different blocks this time. The division block is the next. In the first input, put 'length of a' (which is 1, by the way) just because we can.
   In the second input slot, put the 'pick random' 1 to 2 block. And you are good to go!

Sensing

Wondering how to keep track of time, volume, distance and what your sprite is in contact with? This is the field for that!

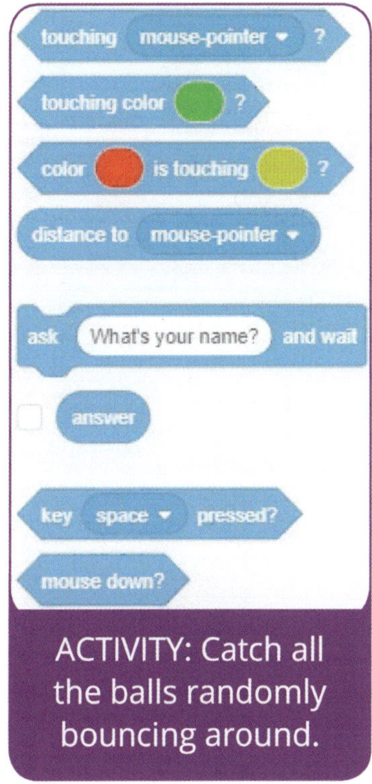

Paddle Game

Learn the sensing blocks by creating this game.

We will use a number of sprites for this game (Ball, Basketball, Beachball, Baseball, Paddle). The good news is that for almost all of them, the entire chunk of code is the same! The backdrop for this one is Night City. Now that we know that, let's get started.

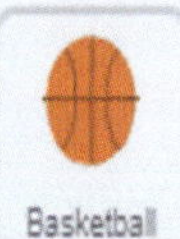

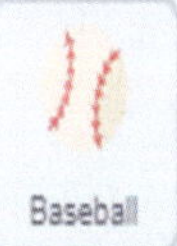

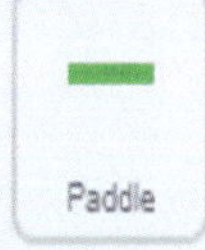

Paddle:

1. As usual, start with the 'when flag clicked' block.

2. From Sensing, look for the 'ask _ and wait' block.

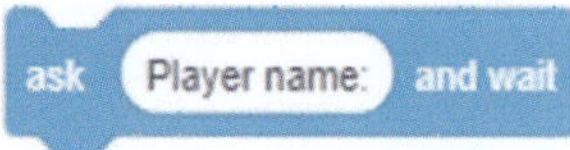

3. Go to Motions and grab the 'set x to' _. Also get the 'set y to' _. (0, -120).

4. Under that, grab the 'say _ for _ seconds'. Duplicate it.

5. In the first one, use a 'join _ _' block from Operators and fill the first entry with Hello and the second one with answer. The answer block is actually a button that provides the answer to the question asked of the user earlier.

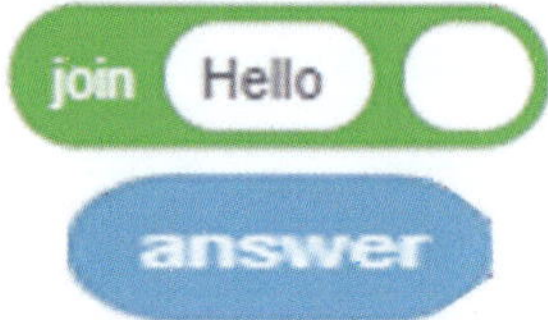

6. For the second one, the input is "Start", 2.

7. And lastly, for this block, add a 'broadcast <message>' to it.

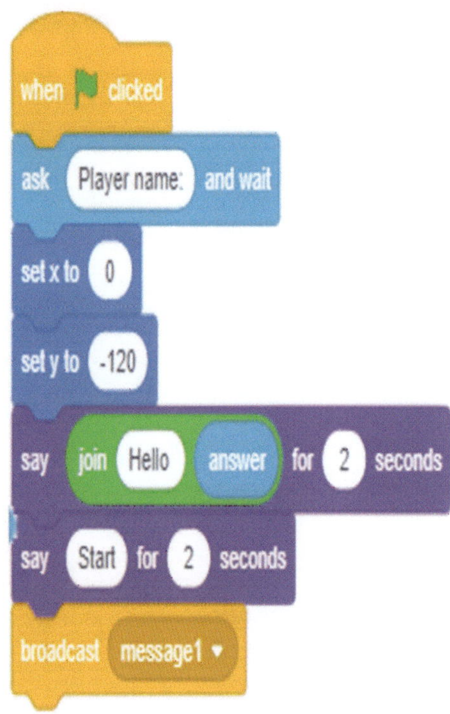

The other sprites:

Ball:

8. Begin with a 'when I receive <message>'. Remember that the name of the message should match the one broadcast in instruction #7.

9. Add a 'show' block from Looks.

10. Go to Events and grab a forever block. The rest of the code will be found nested in it.

11. Get a 'glide _ secs to random position' from Motions. This is the line where the input changes - that is, the time input.

12. Still from Motions, grab the 'if on edge, bounce'.

13. To that, add the 'if _ then' block from Control.

14. The input for the above block is the 'touching <drop-down-list>?'. Select Paddle in the drop-down list.

15. Nest the hide block in the if block.

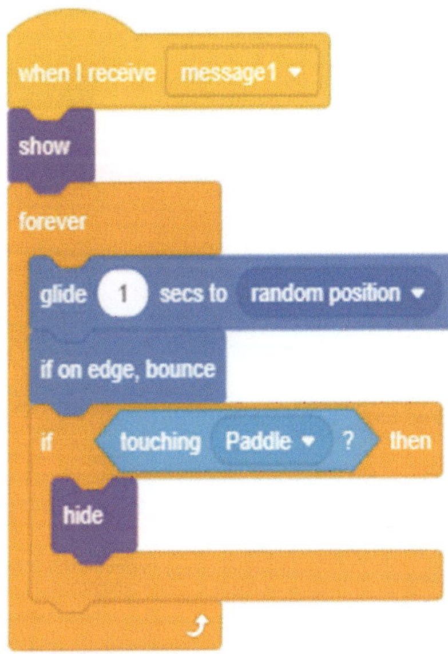

ADDITIONAL BLOCKS FOR THE OTHER SPRITES:

So where there's 1 in the 'glide _ secs to random position', you'll put these in accordingly. All the blocks below are from Operators.

16. BASKETBALL

17. BEACHBALL

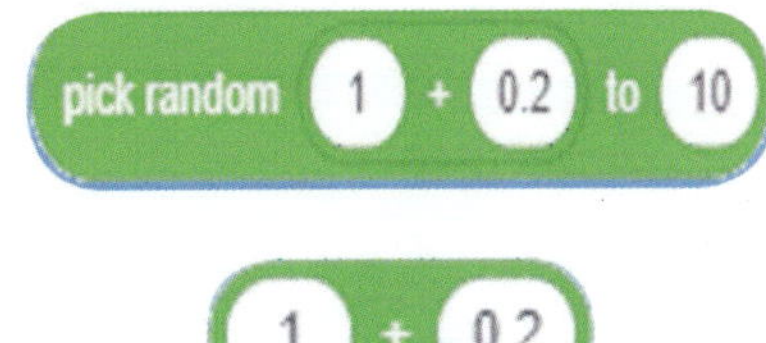

18. BASEBALL

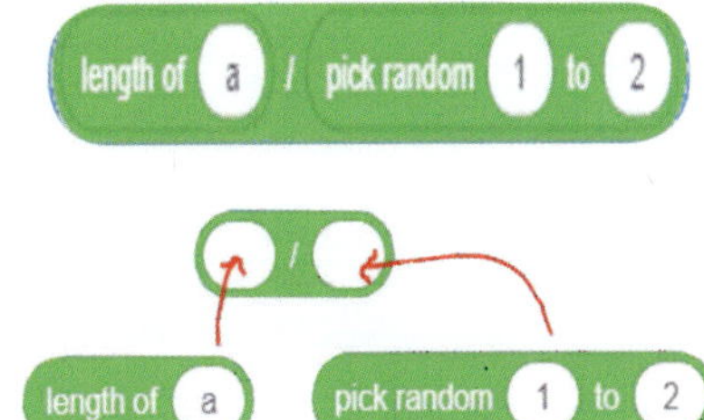

More on Statements

Conditional Statements and Loops

At times, you would like to have blocks of code run only when you want them to, without you having to go and click them. Such statements are called conditional statements.

There are also times when you would like a code to run repeatedly. Maybe run them a set number of times, or even forever. Instead of manually doing so, putting the code in a loop statement would do the job.

Events

So, the title is self explanatory. I should just end here and leave you to handle the rest! Seriously though, the blocks in this section are the ones you use when you are waiting for something specific to happen.

Take a look:

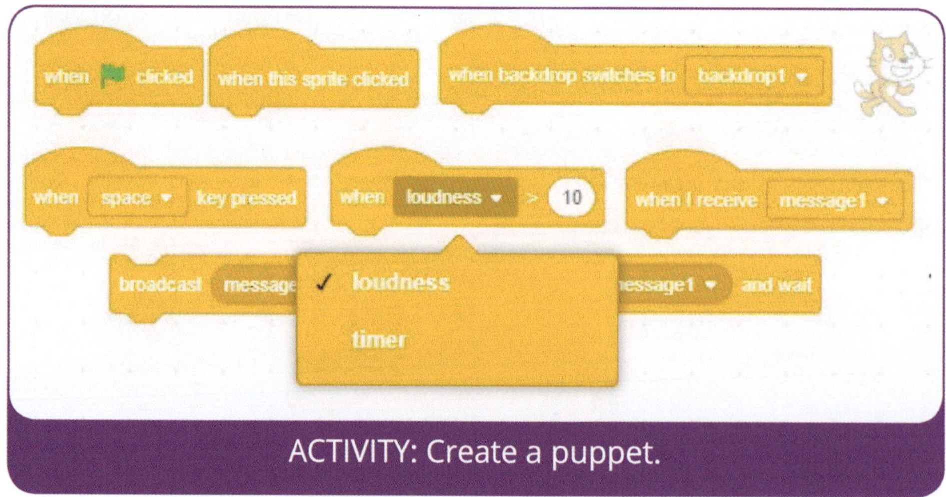

ACTIVITY: Create a puppet.

Puppet Master

Learn to use the events blocks by creating a puppet.

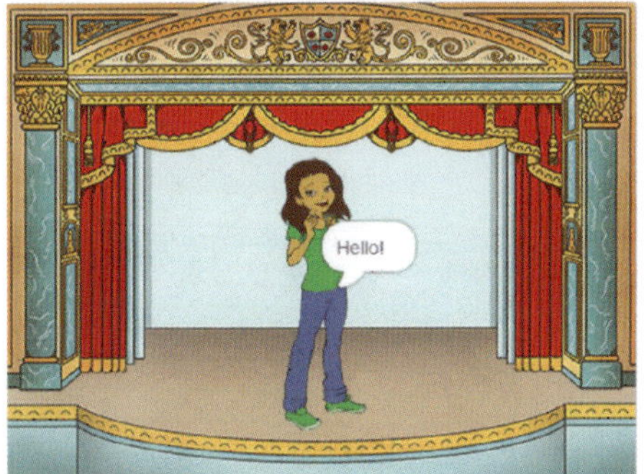

In this game, we'll use just one sprite: "Abby" and one backdrop: "Theater".

Event compilation #1:

1. The first event block we'll use is one we are familiar with. Check it out.

```
when [flag] clicked
switch costume to abby-c ▾
```

2. Next, we use the 'switch costume to abby-c'.
3. Create and duplicate the 'say _ for _ seconds' block so that there are 3 of them. These blocks and the next one all give instructions to the user.

```
say Hello! for 2 seconds
say Here are the instructions. for 2 seconds
say Press the SPACEBAR to quit the instructions for 5 seconds
```

4. Lastly for this pile, we add a 'say _ block'. Notice that this one has no time limit. Remember these blocks can be found in the Looks blocks.

```
say LEFT to move left, RIGHT to move right, S to somersault and D to Dance
```

```
when [flag] clicked
switch costume to abby-c ▾
say Hello! for 2 seconds
say Here are the instructions. for 2 seconds
say Press the SPACEBAR to quit the instructions for 5 seconds
say LEFT to move left, RIGHT to move right, S to somersault and D to Dance
```

Event compilation #2:

5. One of the instructions is for the user to press the spacebar to proceed. This block listens for that event. Look for the 'when _ key pressed'. When you click the drop-down list you'll find the keys it can listen for. In this case, select <space>.

6. At this point, we switch her costume to abby-a.

```
switch costume to abby-a ▾
```

7. And lastly, she will say “Everything clear then! Let us get started!” for 5 seconds.

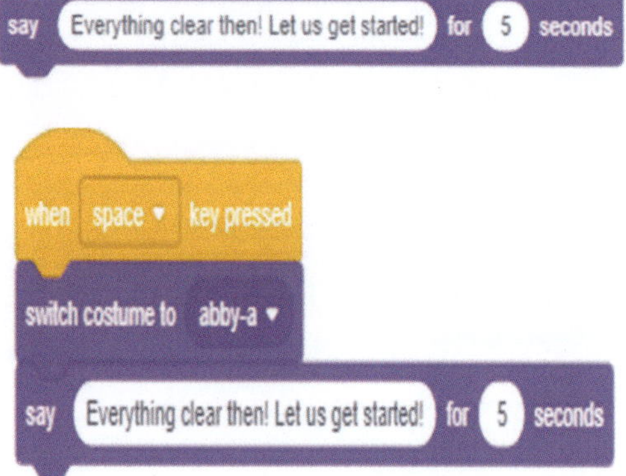

Event compilation #3:

8. We want Abby to somersault when the user presses <s>. For that, we use the 'when _ key pressed' block.

9. We will also use the 'switch costume to _' from Looks 3 different times. The costumes will be abby-d, abby-c and abby-a in that order.

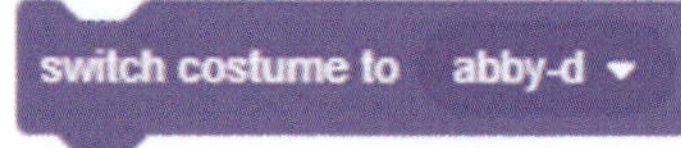

10. So that she doesn’t somersault or change costumes too fast for the human eye, we need 6 'wait _ seconds' blocks.

11. For the actual somersault, lets use the 'turn [backward] 90 degrees' 4 times. We can get this one from the motion blocks. Arrange these blocks as shown below.

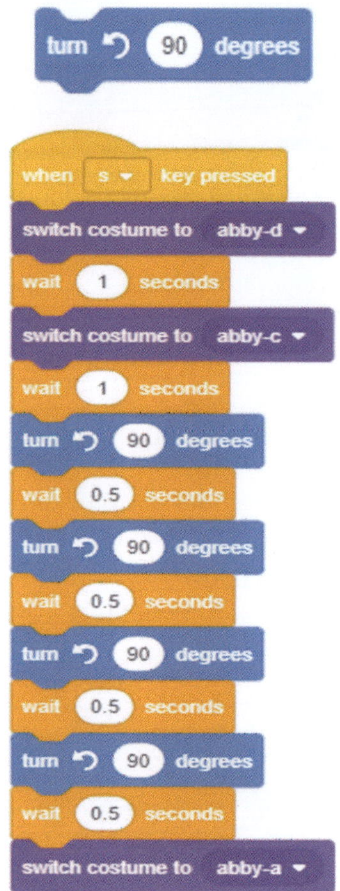

Event compilation #4:

12. Again, we use the 'when ... key pressed' to start this block. See how powerful a block can be? Select <d> in the drop-down list. When a user presses this, Abby begins dancing.

13. The next block is 'repeat [number]'. It can be found in the Control blocks and helps so that the code in it is repeated a specific number of times. Make a duplicate of this block.

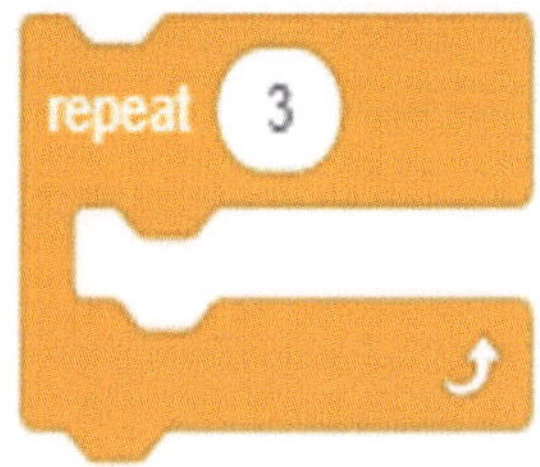

14. Abby will 'switch costume to _' 4 different times (to abby-a, abby-d, abby-b and abby-c) respectively.

15. And for each costume change we want her to 'wait _ seconds' so we can see it!

16. Arrange the blocks as in the bottom right image.

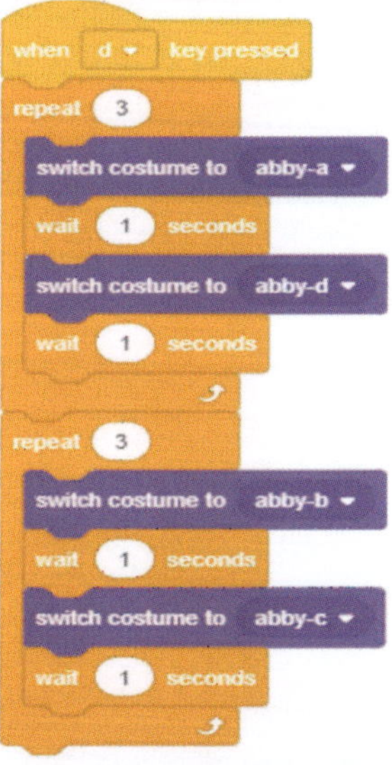

Event compilation #5:

17. When the user presses the right arrow, we want Abby to move in that direction. So we begin with the 'when _ key pressed' and select right arrow in the drop-down list.

18. Add the 'move _ steps' with the value of 10 so that she moves in the right direction. This block belongs to the Motion section.

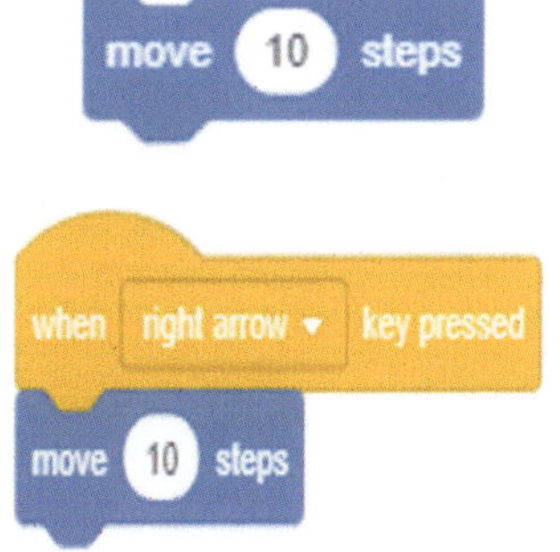

Event compilation #6:

18. Again we use the 'when key pressed' with the value as left arrow, so that this chunk of code is activated when the user presses the left arrow.

19. And again we use the 'move _ steps' block, except this time the value is -10. Think of it as a number line. Positive goes in the right direction and negative in the left direction.

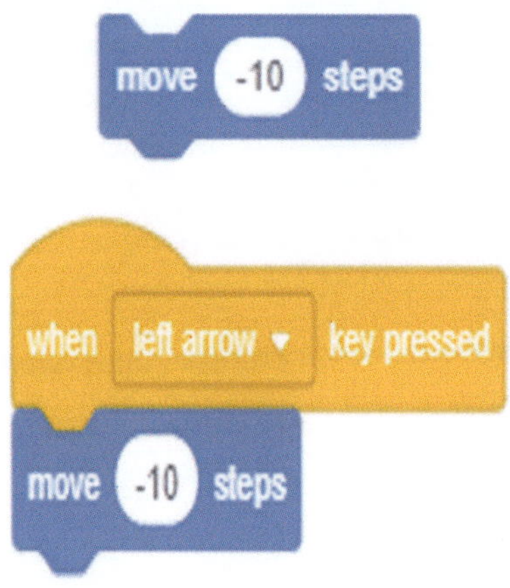

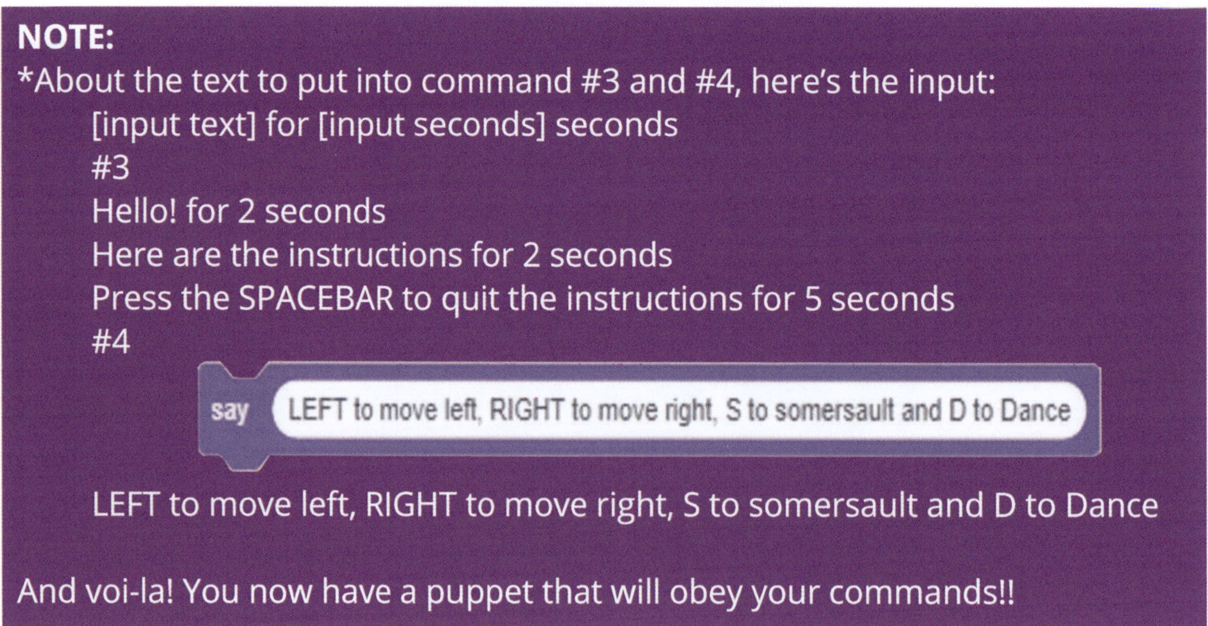

NOTE:

*About the text to put into command #3 and #4, here's the input:

[input text] for [input seconds] seconds

#3

Hello! for 2 seconds

Here are the instructions for 2 seconds

Press the SPACEBAR to quit the instructions for 5 seconds

#4

say LEFT to move left, RIGHT to move right, S to somersault and D to Dance

LEFT to move left, RIGHT to move right, S to somersault and D to Dance

And voi-la! You now have a puppet that will obey your commands!!

Control

While Events focuses on specific... events, control is broader. In what situation do you want a block of code to run, when do you want to pause it or stop it and all that. Control, in fact, includes loops and conditionals.

One thing that you should take note of is the difference in shape between the Events blocks and the Control blocks. Most of the blocks in Control are not starter blocks.

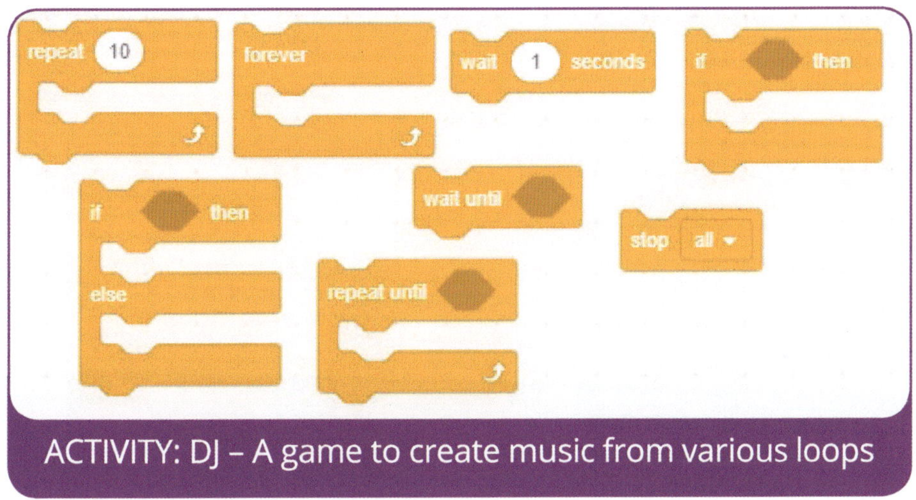

ACTIVITY: DJ – A game to create music from various loops

DJ!!!!

Get familiar with the control blocks by creating a DJ game.

Okay, to get started, we shall use only one sprite: Ruby. And the backdrop is 'Concert'.

Pile #1:

1. To start the game, we will use the usual block Now for the rest of the blocks duplicate them into 2 blocks. The input will be in brackets at the end of each command.

2. Add the 'go to x: _ y: _' ((-175, 102), (0,0))

go to x: -175 y: 102

3. After that, add the 'switch costume to _'. (ruby-b, ruby-a)

switch costume to ruby-b

4. Then get the sprite to 'say _ for _ seconds'. (('Hello', 2), ('Great!', 2))

5. Get the 'repeat until _' block from Control.

6. To the blank spot in the above block, put the 'key [drop-down] pressed'? block from sensing. (key = <space>)

key space pressed?

7. Put the 'say _' block in the 'repeat until'. Thanks to the combo of commands from 5-6, a user can exit the game by pressing the spacebar. (The say content will be found at the end of the game!)

say I have a problem and need your help. Do you mind? Press space

```
when [flag] clicked
go to x: -175 y: 102
switch costume to ruby-b
say Hello! for 2 seconds
repeat until key space pressed?
    say I have a problem and need your help. Do you mind? Pr
switch costume to ruby-a
go to x: 0 y: 0
say Great! for 2 seconds
repeat until key space pressed?
    say So here's the deal: I need some music made for me. I I
```

The Music Loops:

Good news! The code for running the loops isn't hard. While a number of sounds will have to be added to the sprite, the code to run each sound is similar = the only difference is some have the wait statement while others don't. Make one compilation first then duplicate it.

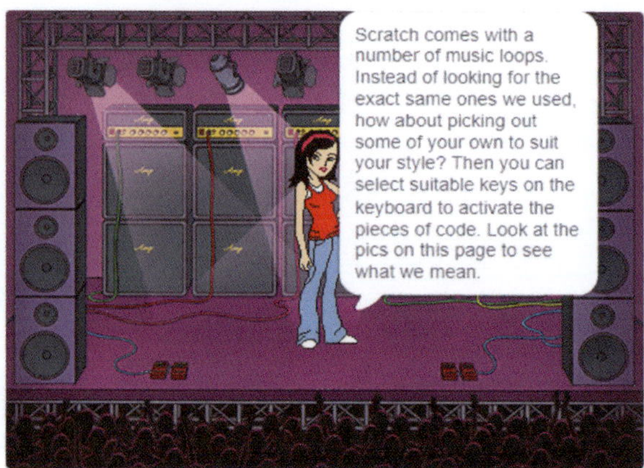

Scratch comes with a number of music loops. Instead of looking for the exact same ones we used, how about picking out some of your own to suit your style? Then you can select suitable keys on the keyboard to activate the pieces of code. Look at the pics on this page to see what we mean.

8. Start with the 'when _ key pressed'.

when c key pressed

9. Add a forever block to it. You can find this one in Control.

forever

10. Get the 'play sound _ until done' block from Sound blocks. Nest it in the forever block.

play sound Hand Clap until done

11. Include the 'wait _ seconds' block in the forever block.

wait 0.5 seconds

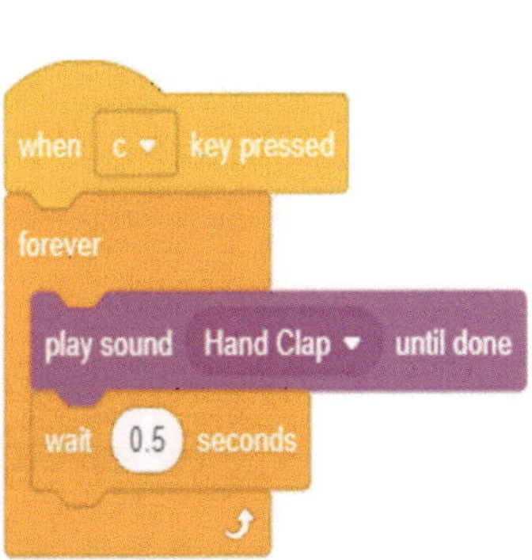
when c key pressed
forever
play sound Hand Clap until done
wait 0.5 seconds

The End game code:

12. To stop the DJ-ing work, we will have to add some more code to the sprite. Look for the 'when this sprite clicked' block in Events.

when this sprite clicked

13. In the Control loops look for the 'stop all' block (It has a drop down list but we don't need the rest for now).

stop all
when this sprite clicked
stop all

INPUT FOR SAY (referred to in instruction #4):
First input: "I have a problem and need your help. Do you mind? Press space to learn more about it. And click me when you would like to stop the game."

Second input: "So here's the deal: I need some music made for me. I have the loops - I just need them mixed. Just press any of these keys to start playing the respective loops
C - Handclap; D - Drip-drop; F - Finger-snap; G - Guitarchord; R - Reggae;
S - Drumset; V - Videogame; X - Xylophone"

Variables and functions

Meaning and Purpose

At times – okay, most of the time – when programming, you want to keep track of some things. How much time has passed, for example since the player started the game? What is their current score? At what score is the game over? That is where variables come into play. Think of them as containers in which you store info.

In the 'DJer' game, most of the sound loop players have basically the same blocks. And we had to copy and paste for every single sound loop we used. That got old fast, didn't it? Now imagine you had to do that for a number of sprites? That is the kind of thing that can make a person go crazy! Functions save you from that hassle. Once you create a function, you can call it (use it) with just a literal block of code. Amazing, right? Just stick with me – you will see just how amazing this can be!

Variables

So before we get to the activity we need to know how to create a variable. After clicking the "Make a Variable" button, this window will appear:

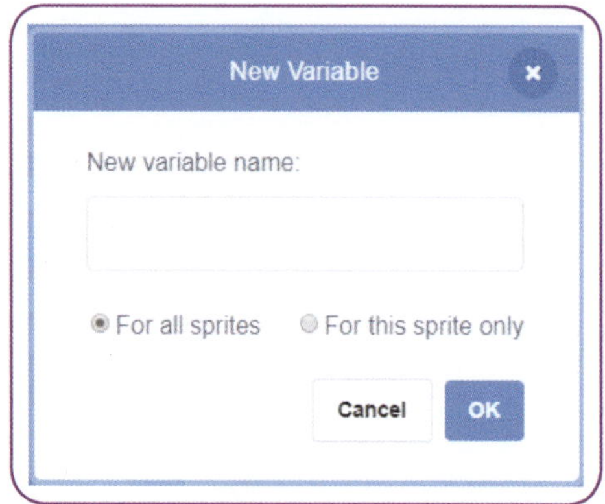

Once you have done so, (the name of the variables I used are 'char_count' and 'Time left') the variables will automatically be added to the drop down lists in the Variables blocks. So now when you want to use that block for a specific variable, just use the drop-down list!

The activity below will show you how you can do so.

ACTIVITY: Game to test typing speed.

Type Speedometer

Let us create a game that measures the typing speed in 2 minutes. In the process we will be more comfortable with variables.

The sprite for this activity is Giga. We will use a backdrop called 'Stars'.

Create a variable:
Clicking the 'Make a variable' button in Variables should lead to a window where you can type the name of the variable. (char_count and Time left for this game). When you click ok, the variable will be added to the drop-down lists of all the blocks in Variables. We will use those blocks in the rest of the code.

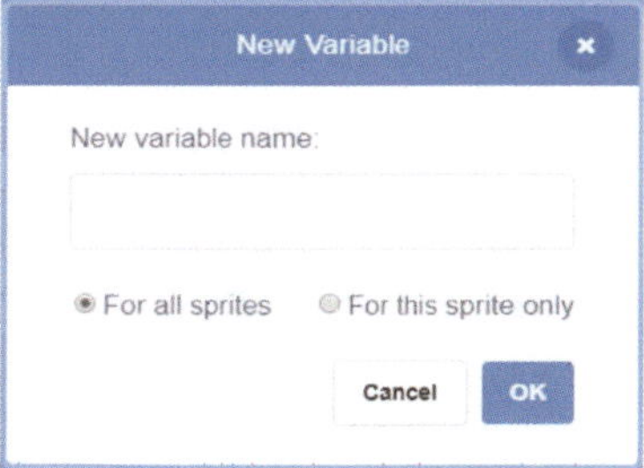

Code to start the program:

1. Same old start with the 'when [flag] clicked'.

2. Create 6 'say _ for _ seconds'. Structure them as the pic to the far right shows.

3. Add a 'repeat until _' block. The input for that will be the key <space> pressed from Sensing.

4. Nest a 'say _' block from Looks in it.

say Press space to get started

5. The rest of the 'say _ for _' blocks come here.
6. Add a 'reset timer' block from sensing.

reset timer

7. Get a 'set <char_count> to 0' from the Variables section.

set char_count to 0

8. Insert a 'broadcast <message1>' block here.

broadcast message1

9. Lastly for this code, add a 'show variable <char_count>' block from Variables.

show variable char_count

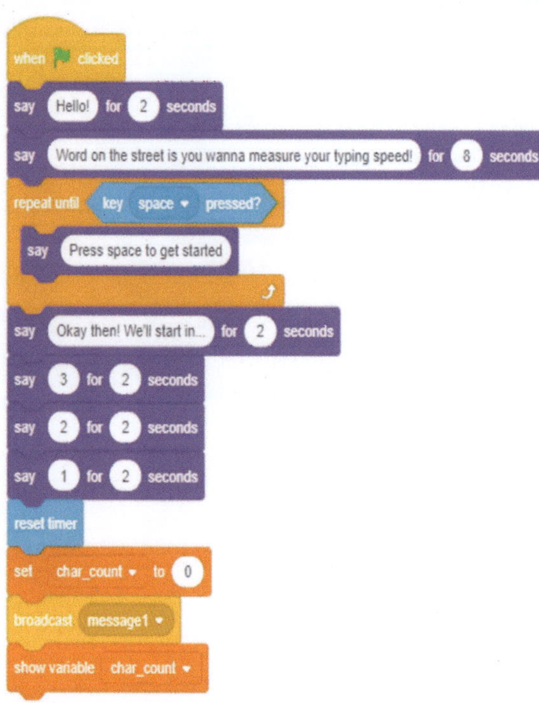

The counter code:

10. Begin this bit with the 'when <any> key pressed' block.
11. Get the 'change <char_count> by 1'.

when any key pressed
change char_count by 1

The counter code:

12. Start with the 'when I receive <message1>' block.

13. The forever block comes next, with the rest coming in it.

14. Put the 'set <Time left> to _'. The input in this line is got by nesting some blocks from operators with one also from Sensing.

15. We will use the 'show variable <Time left>' from Variables.

16. The 'if _ then' block comes next. We use a comparison operator with the Time left button as one input and 2 as the other.

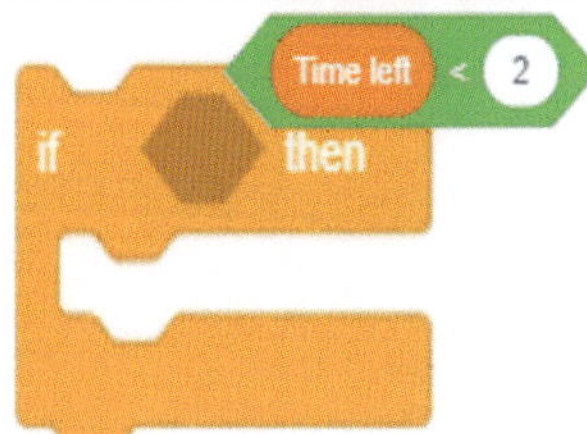

17. In the if block, we put the 'start sound <Referee Whistle>' as a way to alert the player that time is up.

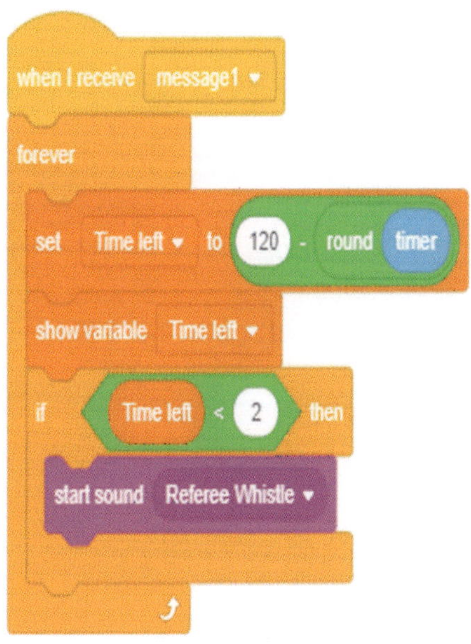

The concluding block:

18. When <timer> > 120 is the code that opens this code.
19. Second is say <Time's up!> for 5 seconds.
20. Then a say join [Your typing speed in characters per second is (char_count/120)].
21. Use the hide variable <drop-down list> to hide char_count and Time left.

My Blocks

This is where you create Scratch's version of a function. The function created can be used only for that sprite, so you will have to drag and drop if you want to use it on other sprites. Now let us take a look at how My Blocks save time!

Gymnast

Now let us learn how to use the My Blocks section by creating an animation.

Just one sprite for this animation: Ten80 Dance. The Backdrop we will use is Hall. We want to create an animation that does somersaults and dances too!

Create dance and somersault blocks:

1. Click the make a block button in My Blocks. The window that pops up should look like this. Replace 'block name' with somersault then click the 'add input' button twice so that 2 slots appear in the block. Fill the first with x=0 and the second with y=0. Click OK. It will create a block like this.

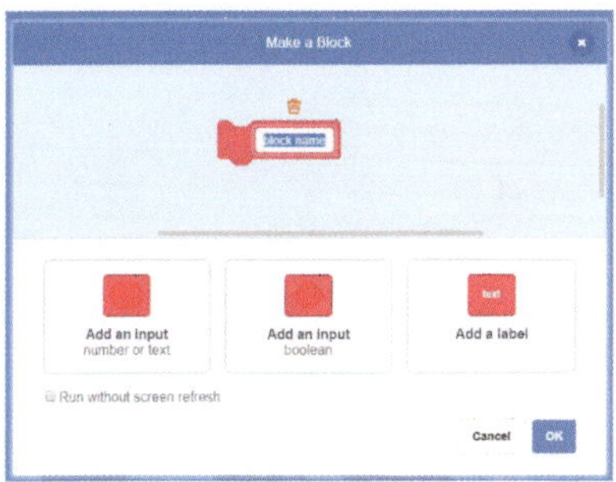

2. Repeat step 1 with the 'block name' of dance.

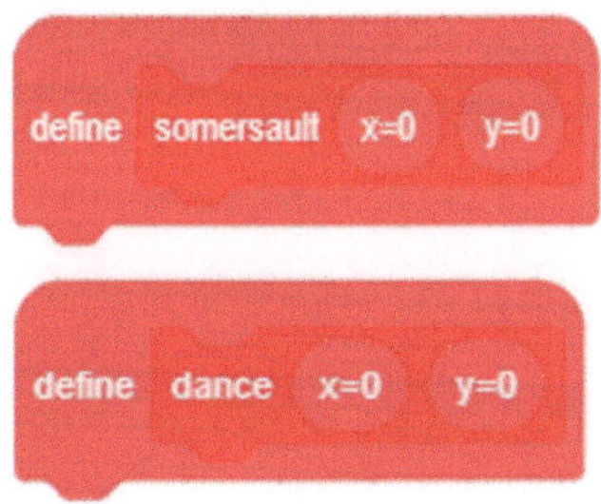

3. Excellent! Now to both of these statements add a 'go to x: _ y: _'. We want the input for these to be from the input in the define block. If you click and drag the x=0 from the define block, you will have a value you can put in the 'go to x: _ y: _' block. Do the same with the input for y, so that it looks like so.

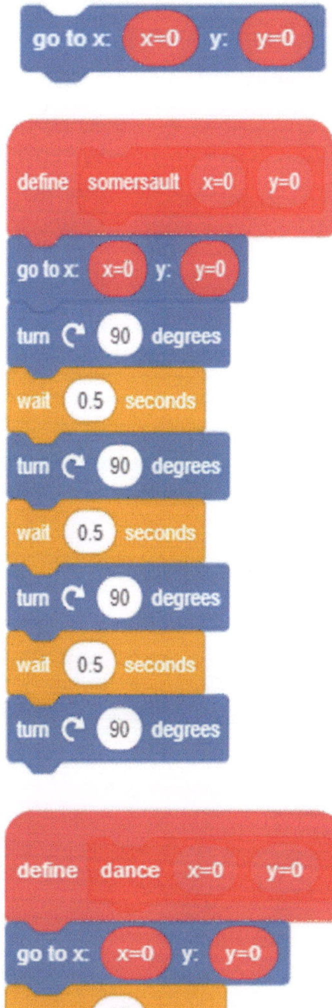

4. We have made sprites somersault and dance before, so you can use that code and attach it to the above blocks. The end result should be as in the previous photo.
5. Now as for the rest of the code, we are going to use the blocks that we have created to make the sprite dance and somersault. Here's the one we created, though you can change the input and order to suit yourself.
6. Notice that since we set x to 0 and y to 0 when creating the blocks, we can run them with no visible entry. Take a look at the third and fourth blocks in our final code.

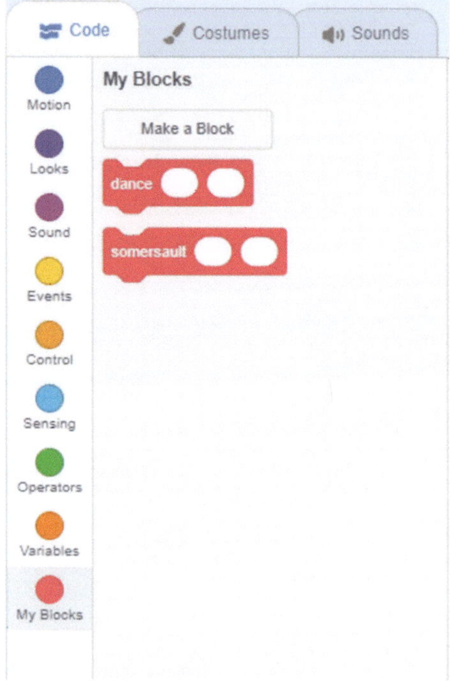

Final Game

You have reached the final game! In this one, you are going to learn how to combine all that you have learned to make a powerful and awesome game! Since the details have already been explained, all that you will see here is the basic blocks.

Ever played a video game before? It doesn't have to be complex – even the ones similar to what we see in some TV shows and sitcoms that I won't mention qualify! So now you are going to create one with the help of yours truly!

Treasure Hunter

For the final game, we are combining all the things we have learnt to create a mermaid treasure hunter. At this point, you don't need our help to prove that to you, we will just provide the blocks. All the instructions are found in the different chapters of this book. Let the game begin!

SPRITES:

BACKDROP:

BLOCK FOR JELLYFISH, CRAB AND HIPPO1:

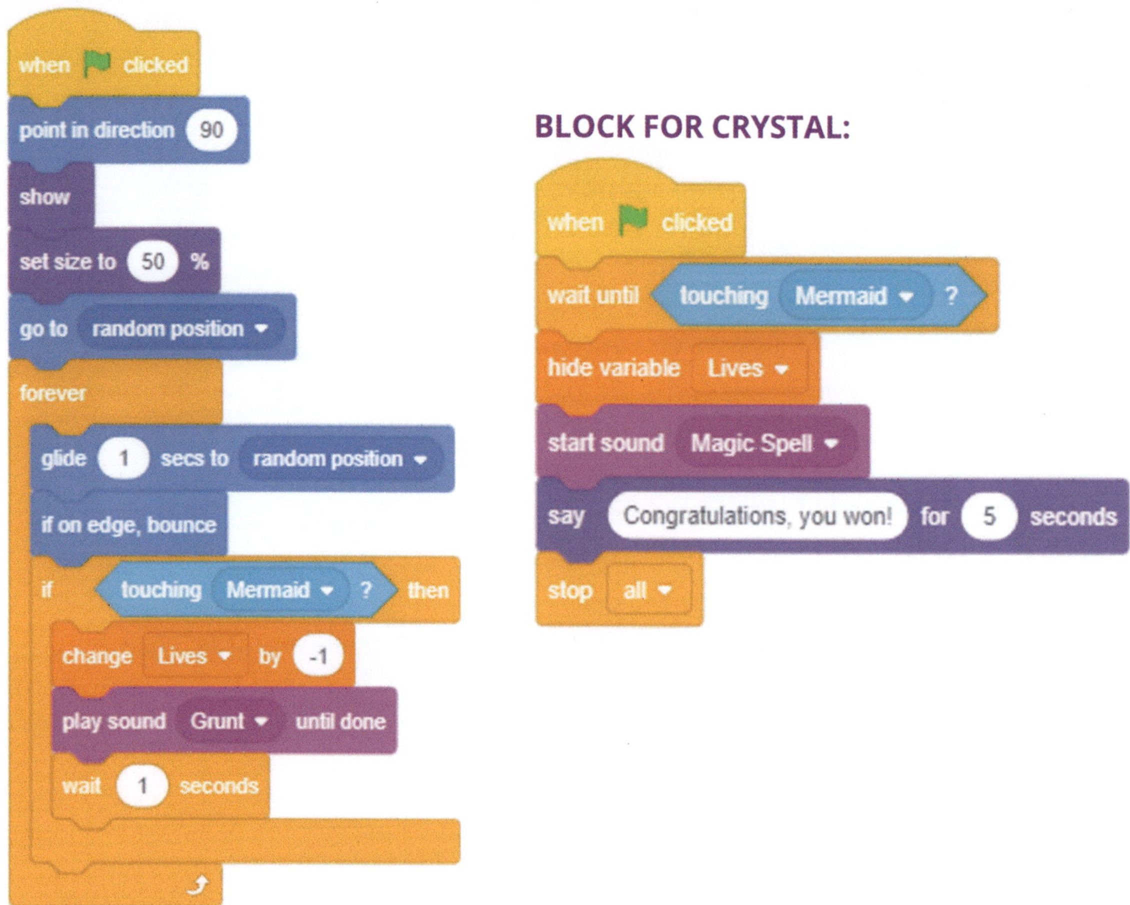
when clicked
point in direction 90
show
set size to 50 %
go to random position
forever
glide 1 secs to random position
if on edge, bounce
if touching Mermaid ? then
change Lives by -1
play sound Grunt until done
wait 1 seconds

BLOCK FOR CRYSTAL:

when clicked
wait until touching Mermaid ?
hide variable Lives
start sound Magic Spell
say Congratulations, you won! for 5 seconds
stop all

Remember that you can share this code across all sprites by dragging and dropping into the sprites.

For the 'play sound __ until done' block, the sound is 'GRUNT' for Hippo1, chomp for crab and also Hippo1.

CODE OF THE MERMAID SPRITE

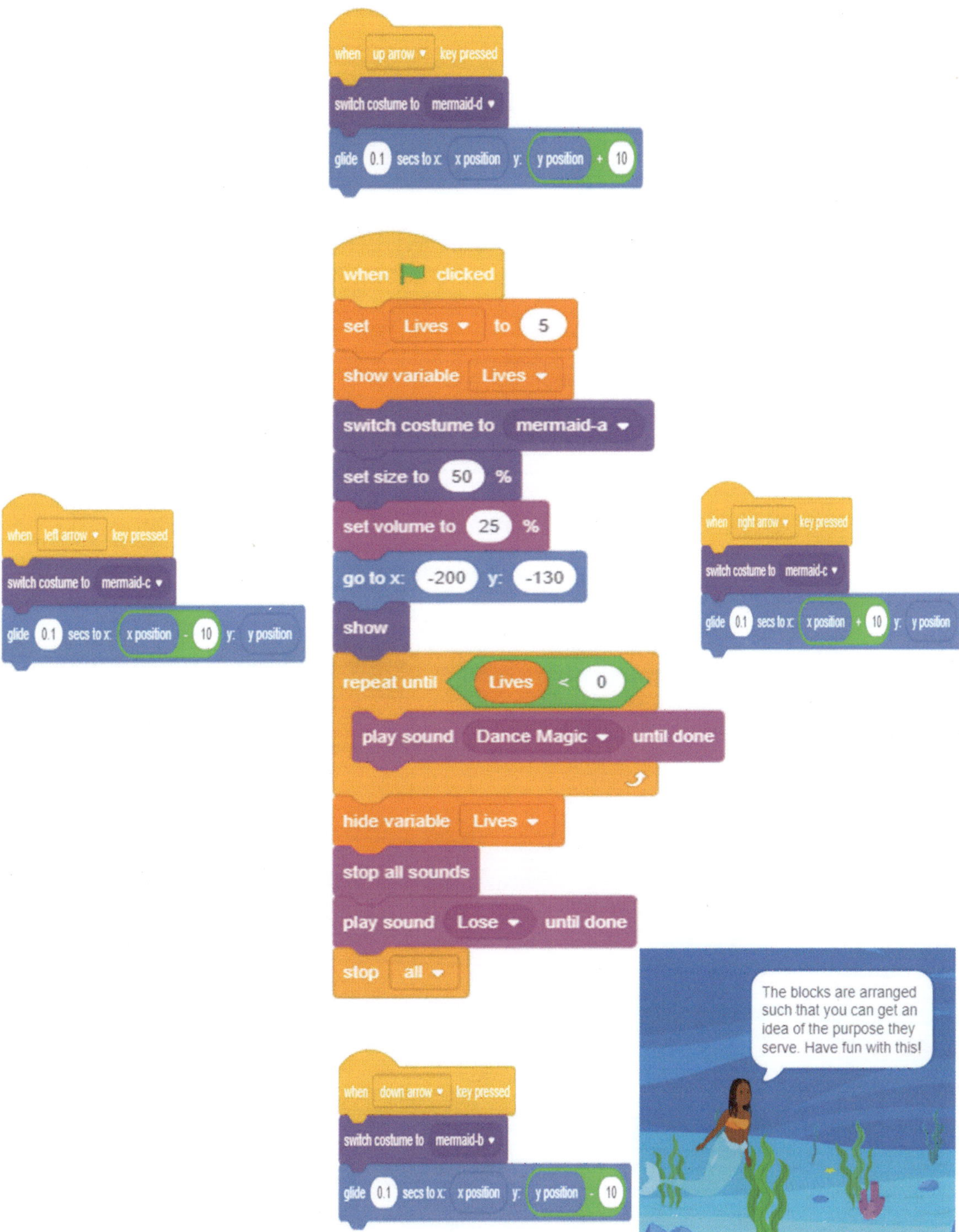

when up arrow key pressed
switch costume to mermaid-d
glide 0.1 secs to x: x position y: y position + 10
when clicked
set Lives to 5
show variable Lives
switch costume to mermaid-a
set size to 50 %
set volume to 25 %
go to x: -200 y: -130
show
repeat until Lives < 0
play sound Dance Magic until done
hide variable Lives
stop all sounds
play sound Lose until done
stop all
when left arrow key pressed
switch costume to mermaid-c
glide 0.1 secs to x: x position - 10 y: y position
when right arrow key pressed
switch costume to mermaid-c
glide 0.1 secs to x: x position + 10 y: y position
when down arrow key pressed
switch costume to mermaid-b
glide 0.1 secs to x: x position y: y position - 10
The blocks are arranged such that you can get an idea of the purpose they serve. Have fun with this!

Congratulations! You are now proficient at Scratch! Weird how using certain words adds gravity to the sentence, isn't it?

Trying to figure out what to do next, though? Well for starters, why not try to create a few games or animations on your own? The ones here are really simple, so I am sure that as you were going through them, you came up with ways to improve them.

Plus, you could try out ideas of your own – create a game from scratch, so to speak (see what I did there? Lol.) If your creative juices are running low, you could always go to Scratch for some of theirs.

Just click the "Ideas" button at the top of the home page once you have logged in.

Scratch, awesome as it is, is not the end of the road. As mentioned earlier, it will make it easier for you to learn other programming languages. Like, for example, Python. Weird, did I just say Python? Such a coincidence! Seriously, because the next book in this series introduces you to Python! Why not check it out?

Join the WIZKIDS CLUB

Enter today and win a FREE BOOK!

Do you have any travel adventure stories or project ideas you want share with me? Yes? Great! You can mail me at my id and become a member of the WIZKIDS CLUB!

www.wizkidsclub.com

Write to me at: sumita@wizkidsclub.com